What people are

Personalities in the Pews

"In his sharing of these stories, we see a pastor's heart and grace. Eldon Irving offers us a portrait of humanity that is real: sometimes funny, sometimes painful or even maddening, but always the portrait is painted through eyes of grace.

"This book will make you think, laugh and occasionally bring a tear to your eye. I commend it to you as a celebration of humanity and of God's redemptive work in and through us."

> The Rev. Dr. Richard L. Hamm
> Former General Minister and President
> Christian Church (Disciples of Christ)
> Author of *2020 Vision for the Christian Church (Disciples of Christ)*

"Eldon Irving's book depicts a hopeful reality, one that avoids the cynicism that often infects the church's life. All readers in the church will enjoy these vignettes. More important, all will learn something new, and catch within these pages a glimpse of what it really means to be Christian in today's world."

> Dr. Mark G. Toulouse
> Professor of American Religious History
> Brite Divinity School, Texas Christian University
> Author of *God in Public: Four Ways American Christianity and Public Life Relate*

About the Author and Illustrator

Eldon Irving served in the ministry for forty-three years, the last twenty-eight years as senior pastor of First Christian Church in Duncanville, Texas, a suburb of Dallas.

Born in McAllen, Texas, Dr. Irving graduated Phi Beta Kappa and Magna Cum Laude from the University of Washington. He received additional degrees from Yale University, United Theological Seminary, Brite Divinity School at Texas Christian University, and did graduate study at the University of Edinburgh in Scotland.

Dr. Irving has been active in the Christian Church (Disciples of Christ) at the area, regional, and general levels. He served on the Committee of Recommendations to the International Convention of Christian Churches, has been a member of the General Board of the Christian Church, served on the Worship Commission for the General Church, served on the Ohio Youth Commission, and was moderator of the North Texas Area of the Christian Church in the Southwest.

Dr. Irving's published works include a book, *The Life of Christ in Masterpieces of Art;* articles in Yale Divinity School's magazine, denominational magazines, and *Reader's Digest;* and newspapers in Ohio, Colorado, and Texas.

After having served churches in Warren and Dayton, Ohio, and Kansas City, Kansas, Dr. Irving began his ministry in Duncanville, Texas, in 1976. In the course of his twenty-eight-year ministry in Duncanville, the church was recognized by the National Evangelical Association for "excellence in evangelism and church growth." The church building doubled in size, the budget was increased by more than 700 percent, many new programs and ministries were added, and the church was recognized by the General Assembly as one of five Christian Churches in the United States for being an "exemplary teaching congregation."

As this book went to press, Dr. Irving was informed that he had been chosen by Brite Divinity School at Texas Christian University to receive the Distinguished Minister's Award for Pastoral Ministry. This award is given to only one person each year.

For recreation, Dr. Irving enjoys sailboat racing, and he and his wife, Gloria, have raced in several national regattas. Eldon also is interested in antique cars and for several years made his pastoral calls in a 1929 Model A Roadster.

Gloria Irving studied art at the Kansas City Art Institute, Kansas State University, and received her degree in Fine Arts from the University of Texas at Arlington. She has worked as an artist for Hallmark Cards, a designer for Kevore Wall Coverings in California, an artist at Gill Studio near Kansas City, and an animation artist for K. & H. Productions in Dallas, Texas. For recreation, she enjoys smocking, quilting, and gardening.

Eldon and Gloria have traveled in many countries, and since retirement, they do volunteer work in state parks in the United States.

They have two grown children: Angela and Ryan.

To Virginia,

Best wish

Aug 23, 2011

Personalities in the Pews

(Stories of Inspiration and Humor)

The Rev. Dr. Eldon L. Irving

Eldon L. Irving

Illustrated by Gloria A. Irving

Gloria A. Irving

INFINITY
PUBLISHING

Copyright © 2010 by Eldon L. Irving and Gloria A. Irving
Front cover photo by Bob Cawthon
Back cover photo by Angela Irving
Illustrated chiropractic symbol used by permission.
Illustrated chalice symbol used by permission.

Bible quotations are from the New Revised Standard Version Bible, copyright 1989, Division of Christian Education of the National Council of the Churches of Christ in the United States of America. Used by permission. All rights reserved.

ISBN 0-7414-6169-2

Printed in the United States of America

Published November 2010

INFINITY PUBLISHING
1094 New DeHaven Street, Suite 100
West Conshohocken, PA 19428-2713
Toll-free (877) BUY BOOK
Local Phone (610) 941-9999
Fax (610) 941-9959
Info@buybooksontheweb.com
www.buybooksontheweb.com

For

Gloria

Acknowledgments

Appreciation for:
The personalities in the pews of the churches I served:
Central Christian Church in Warren, Ohio; Hillcrest
Christian Church in Dayton, Ohio; Central Christian Church
in Kansas City, Kansas; and First Christian Church in
Duncanville, Texas.

Thanks to:
Dick Hamm for writing the foreword;
Reid Huntley, Mark Toulouse, and Alan Elliott for reading
the manuscript, making suggestions, and writing reviews;
Robin Sanders, Ryan Irving, and Bill Faulkner for help with
computer matters;
Bob Cawthon for the front cover photo;
Angela Irving for the back cover photo; and
Gloria, my wife, for illustrating the book and being a constant,
loving companion.

Table of Contents

Foreword by The Rev. Dr. Richard L. Hamm   i

Introduction   iii

1. The Ice-cream Man Cometh   1
2. The Inspiration of Spunk   5
3. An Invincible Spirit   9
4. Getting the Word   13
5. More than Cowboy Boots   17
6. The Dirty Old Man   23
7. The Man of Many Talents   27
8. The Computer Angel   31
9. A Shiny Red Suit and a Song   37
10. The Extended Pew   41
11. The Rumble-seat Pew   47
12. The Sweet Sister Gambit   53
13. The Main Event   57
14. Responses to Preaching   63
15. The Worshiping Pew   67

16. The Organ Pew   71

17. The First Women Elders   75

18. God Bless the Youth Sponsors   79

19. Baptized in the Water   85

20. The Welcome Table   89

21. The Hospital Pew   95

22. The Counseling Pew   99

23. For Better or For Worse   103

24. From the Pew to the Gravesite   109

25. Let the Little Children Come   113

26. The Family Pew   117

27. Each in Her Own Pew   121

28. More than Pew Sitters   125

29. That Special Ingredient   137

30. God's Greatest Gift to Me   143

31. My Wife's Best-Kept Secret   147

32. Epilogue: The Other Side of the Story   151

Index of Personalities in the Pews   155

Index of Scriptures   159

Foreword

One of the things I have always loved about congregational ministry is watching and listening to the choir on a Sunday morning as they sing an anthem beautifully or not so beautifully. As a pastor, I have known the story of most every member who ever sang in the choir of a congregation I was serving. Sooner or later, I would come to know their strengths and weaknesses, their successes and failures. I have always been touched by watching these imperfect people, some near-saints but more sinners and often downright colorful characters who sing the Gospel from their hearts. It is a special embodiment of grace.

Reading *Personalities in the Pews* is much the same experience. The characters in this book will be recognized by every minister and by every lay church leader. The names may be different from those of the people we have actually known, but the personalities, their gifts, their graces, their excesses and their foibles will all be familiar.

In his sharing of these stories, we see a pastor's heart and grace. Eldon Irving offers us a portrait of humanity that is real: sometimes funny, sometimes painful or even maddening. But always the portrait is painted through eyes of grace, eyes that see like the eyes of Christ see: eyes that see the best and the worst, yet eyes that always hope for the best and always search out God's redemptive work in progress.

Eldon Irving and I became fast friends when I began as his associate in 1974 in Kansas City, Kansas. Though there were many wonderful people at Central Christian Church, it was in many ways a troubled congregation struggling to deal with rapid change that was occurring all around it. It was an extremely difficult ministry for both Eldon and me. Yet I have no regrets for having served there. As a young minister just out of seminary, I learned so much from Eldon who became a marvelous mentor. We have remained friends through the years, and I have always been grateful for his grace, wisdom and guidance in those early days of my ministry and found that what I learned from him has held up well. He has both a pastor's heart and a pastor's head: a powerful combination that has touched the lives of so many.

This book will make you think, laugh and occasionally bring a tear to your eye. I commend it to you as a celebration of humanity and of God's redemptive work in and through us.

The Rev. Dr. Richard L. Hamm
Former General Minister and President
Christian Church (Disciples of Christ)

Introduction

Every Sunday, the pews in a local church hold people who come to worship. In the forty-three years I have been a pastor in the Christian Church (the last twenty-eight years at First Christian Church in Duncanville, Texas—a suburb of Dallas), I have had the opportunity to minister to many colorful personalities in the pews. Some have had the freshness of youth; others have had the wisdom of age. Some were endowed with great intellectual talents, which they shared; others gave of themselves emotionally. Some enjoyed the blessings of good health; others wrestled with the challenge of broken health. As diverse as these personalities were, they all had one thing in common: they all sat as laypersons in the pews of the church. And, as they responded to the worship and to the ministry of the church, all of them in one way or another shared their faith and were an inspiration to the lives they touched. These are their stories.

1

The Ice-cream Man Cometh

Ernest Weatherly had worked all his life for an ice-cream factory, but even long after he was retired from the factory, he had an emotional attachment to it. He loved ice cream, and he loved to give it away, especially to the preacher. Every Saturday morning, he would knock on my door with a gallon of ice cream in his hands and a big grin on his face. If he heard we were having relatives visit or overnight guests, he would bring two gallons. As he stood there every Saturday with his various flavored presents and a big jolly smile, he looked a little like Santa Claus. He didn't wear a red suit, but his plump physical presence matched St. Nick's, which showed he not only liked giving away ice cream, but he also liked eating it.

This "ice-creaming" the minister had been going on for as long as anyone in the church could remember. I loved it, but my predecessor either didn't have a fondness for ice cream or he ate it much more slowly. I am told that at every covered-dish dinner at the church he brought two gallons of ice cream, and when he left to go to another parish, his freezer was full of nothing but ice cream.

Mr. Weatherly was not only a gift giver of ice cream, but he was a gift giver of himself. Not only was he in church every Sunday with his warm countenance and extended hand, but he was also present at every funeral to offer comforting words and support. Since he was an elder emeritus, he was also a permanent member of the official board, and I appreciated his calming presence more than once. I remember one time in particular when someone on the board was upset about something (trivial as I remember it), but it looked like sides were about to be drawn as tension mounted. All of a sudden, Mr. Weatherly pulled out of his pocket two finger puppets and began playing with them as if they were having an argument with each other. Everyone began to laugh, and the tension relaxed as the trivial issue was seen for what it was.

Mr. Weatherly lived in one of the smallest houses owned by members of the congregation, and his income was a modest pension from the ice-cream factory and Social Security, but he was very generous with his money, which he faithfully placed in the offering plate every Sunday. If most of the others had been as generous proportionally as Mr. Weatherly, the church would never have been short of funds for church programming and mission work. Unfortunately, that was not always the case. I remember one time when the offering was running behind, and I shared this with the congregation, asking if those in the pews might be able to give a little more so we could catch up financially. The announcement was aimed at those who were giving very little and could easily give more, but after the service, Mr. Weatherly, who was already tithing (giving ten percent of his income), came up to me and said, "Preacher, I heard what you said. I can give a little more each week." To me, as a pastor, Mr. Weatherly was an inspiration and in many ways gave much more than ice cream.

2

The Inspiration of Spunk

"Preacher, you need to speak up! I come here to hear a sermon and all you do is mumble!"

That was a comment often made by Stella Shinn as she went through the line after the sermon. Mrs. Shinn was well into her nineties and was hard of hearing, but when I suggested she use the hearing aids we provided for the service, she would have none of it.

"There's nothing wrong with my hearing!" she exclaimed. "You just need to speak up."

What Mrs. Shinn lacked in hearing she more than made up for in spunk, and she brought a smile to the face of almost everyone in the church. She was a tiny lady with black and silver hair tightly braided and rolled up in a bun. Her face had age wrinkles, but you had to look fast to see them because she was always on the go.

One day Mrs. Shinn went to the neighbor next door and asked if she could borrow his saw in order to cut some limbs off the tree in her front yard.

"Mrs. Shinn, I'll be happy to cut those limbs off," he offered.

"If I wanted you to cut the limbs off, I would have asked you," she snapped. "Now, can I borrow your saw?"

On another occasion, Mrs. Shinn was scheduled to go with some other ladies in the church to visit people in a nursing home. Prior to the visit, she fell and broke her kneecap. I visited her in her home to see how she was doing, and when I offered to say a prayer, she said with a grin, "OK, but don't expect me to get on my knees."

In spite of her broken kneecap, Mrs. Shinn went with the ladies to the nursing home. I asked her how it went.

"OK, I guess," she said, "but I'm not going back. The place is full of old people, and they just sit there and do nothing. It's depressing."

Probably everyone in the nursing home was younger than Mrs. Shinn.

Mrs. Shinn was part of a group of ladies in the church who got together each week to make quilts. It was mainly for fellowship, but they did offer their finished quilts for sale. I would stop in each week just to say hello. One day, my wife, Gloria, came with me and commented to the ladies how nice it was that they were keeping alive the art of quilt making. She also said she might like to have a quilt made some day. She was standing right next to Mrs. Shinn who apparently interpreted this as an invitation to her and her alone.

The next day Mrs. Shinn telephoned Gloria, "I'm starting your quilt. What color do you want?" She also announced her project to the rest of the group, commenting, "The preacher's wife asked me to do it, not you all." The quilt was done in record time, and it was beautiful.

"How much do I owe you, Mrs. Shinn?" Gloria asked.

"One hundred dollars," she answered.

Gloria knew that a handmade quilt was worth much more than that, so she wrote out a check for more. Mrs. Shinn didn't look at the check until the next day, but when she did, she went straight to Gloria and gave back the extra. "I said one hundred dollars!" she exclaimed. As I said, the quilt was beautiful, and we did manage to get a picture of Mrs. Shinn holding the quilt, although she fussed about having her picture taken.

Mrs. Shinn drove a 1952 white Chevrolet, which from time to time would just quit running, but that didn't stop her from running. If the car didn't go, she walked...briskly. She was in church every Sunday, even during bad weather. Once, we had a terrible ice storm on a Saturday night, and I was expecting a low attendance Sunday morning. My expectation was correct, but even though many younger people felt the weather was too bad to get out, Mrs. Shinn was there.

"It was too dangerous to drive," she said, "so I walked."

That was the Sunday there were so few in church that I said to the small remnant, "Instead of staying in our pews as we normally do during communion and being served by the deacons, many of whom are not here, let me invite you all to come stand around the communion table. As you receive the communion tray, it will be your responsibility to serve those around you...being sure no one is left out. In effect this is a symbol of what we are always to do as Christians...be aware of those around us and be sure no one is left out."

Those who were there that day still talk about how meaningful the experience was. Incidentally, Mrs. Shinn was standing right next to me, and this Sunday she didn't complain about not hearing.

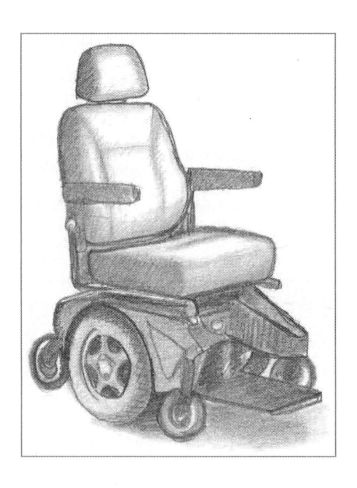

3

An Invincible Spirit

I watched Jason grow up in the church. He was like most of the other young boys, except he was a little more awkward. He would stumble and fall a lot, which caused the other kids, not so much in church but at school, to tease him. Jason took it good-naturedly and even joked about it himself. As the years went on, Jason's awkwardness and stumbling grew worse, and after some medical tests, the doctor discovered he had muscular dystrophy.

By the time Jason was in high school, he was in a wheelchair, but he still took it good-naturedly. In fact, he became very popular because of his positive attitude and his winsome smile. When he advanced to needing a motorized wheelchair, girls would ride on the arm of it up and down the halls in school, and friends were always gathering at his house. Jason was a good listener, and kids of both genders gravitated to him with their adolescent problems.

Because of Jason's medical condition, there was always some new complication arising, and he spent a lot of time in the hospital. As a minister, I visited people in the hospital all the time, and often I would see people with deteriorating conditions get depressed or even bitter, but that was not the case with Jason. He had developed a strong faith, which not only supported him personally, but also encouraged all those around him. His nurses and doctors were constantly telling me what an inspirational patient he was.

When things went wrong, in or out of the hospital, Jason met them with good humor and even joked about them. One such case was at the high-school prom. Jason's dad, Buddy, drove Jason and his date to the prom because their van had a special motorized lift for the wheelchair. After the prom, he picked them up, but Jason wanted to take his date home himself. She lived in the next block, and there was sidewalk all the way with cutouts in the curb, so she hopped on the arms of the wheelchair and they wheeled off. He was gone for some time, but his parents didn't worry, thinking the two probably sat outside her house and talked. It was a beautiful moonlit night.

What happened was this: On his way back home, Jason's battery to his wheelchair ran down, and he couldn't get up the ramp to the house. He called and whistled but neither penetrated the walls of the house. Finally, after what must have seemed like several hours to Jason, his mom, Lyn, went outside to check, and found Jason sitting there alone in the moonlight. She felt terrible that she hadn't checked earlier, but Jason laughed and said, "I'm just glad it didn't rain. It might seem a bit odd to return a rented tuxedo that is completely soaked."

Jason was not only well liked by everyone, but he was also a good student. After he graduated from high school, he headed for Texas A&M. By now, his muscular dystrophy had worsened to the point that he needed to have someone with him to help with the personal necessities of life, but Jason continued to excel in school and was on the dean's list.

While at A&M Jason met a girl named Christina, and they fell in love. When Jason decided to propose, he made a big production of it. With his connections and winsome smile, he managed to get the coach to open up the press box at the football stadium. Christina was sent on a treasure hunt getting clues which sent her to various places and finally to the press box. There was Jason with a ring and a proposal along with a television crew from the local television station.

They were married in the Catholic Church because she was Roman Catholic. The Catholic Deacon and I jointly performed the service. Incidentally, some time later Christina entered a Valentine's Day contest that was looking for the most romantic proposal, and for her story, she won a diamond necklace.

After Jason graduated from A&M with honors, he entered the PhD program in psychology. By this time, he was constantly on a breathing machine, his conversation being interrupted as he took a breath in the middle of each sentence. He also could no longer write with his hand, and had to use a voice-activated computer. With all these challenges, Jason finished his degree, and I was invited to be a part of a big party to celebrate the graduation of Dr. Jason Boles. He was then offered a position at the University of Texas Southwest Medical Hospital.

There are many stories I could relate about Jason. My favorite is this: Once, Jason's friends took him with them to the swimming pool. They carried him to the shallow end where he could sit and feel the water. They would go off and swim and come back constantly to check on him. During this time, an elderly gentleman near the edge of the pool watched all this. Finally, he walked up to Jason and said, "I've been watching, and I noticed you can't move very much. I don't know what happened to you, but I just want to say to you, God will reward you and bless you."

Jason smiled and said, "He already has."

In the middle of a September night in 2002, something went wrong with Jason's breathing machine, and at the age of thirty-seven, the world lost one of the most gentle, creative, and inspirational personalities in the pews. However, to paraphrase a popular maxim: Life is not measured by the number of breaths we take, but by the number of inspirational people who take our breath away.

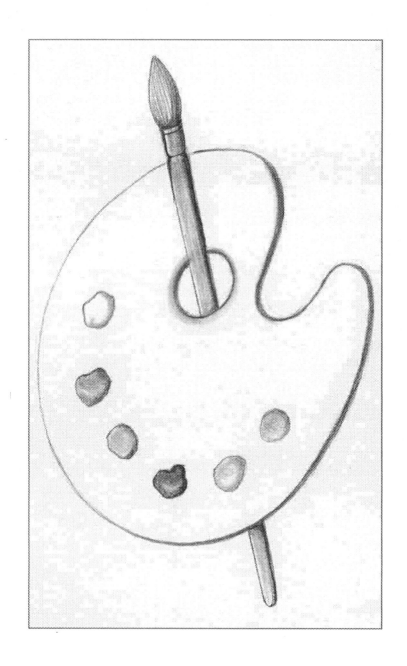

4

Getting the Word

The spoken word gets a lot of attention in seminary. After all, preaching is one of the main roles of a minister. Rena Hansen, however, introduced me to another dimension of "the Word." Rena was an artist. She had been a pew-sitting member of the first church I served after I graduated from seminary (I came as the associate minister), but long before I came, the senior minister there had recognized in her some great leadership ability and had invited her to serve as Christian education director.

I first met Rena right after I graduated, when the church was looking me over and I was looking the church over. Rena invited me to her home for dinner, so we could get acquainted and she could tell me about the church.

Rena, however, was much more interested in the talking part than she was about the dinner part, as she announced, "I was planning on fixing a casserole, but I got tied up at church talking to some people. How do you like baloney sandwiches?"

"Fine," I said, and she motioned me to follow her into the kitchen. In the kitchen, there were murals of happy dancing boys and girls she had painted on each of the cabinet doors, and Rena herself reflected this same image, as she danced about fixing the sandwiches and talking all the time.

"What did you like best about seminary? What kind of church position are you looking for? You'll like it here. There are some really fine people in this congregation."

In the years that I served there, I found Rena's comment about fine people to be true, but there was none finer than Rena herself. Rena was what I call a natural theologian. She had not been to seminary, but she read constantly, had a sharp mind, and loved the give-and-take of talking theology. Having that same interest, we meshed and got along great.

However, Rena had one quality that I did not have...an artistic talent and a keen awareness of the importance of art in the area of the Christian faith.

"Why is it," she would ask, "that most churches today have blank walls? All throughout history the church has been the patron of the arts, and some of the greatest presentations of the Christian faith have been through the medium of art. But today you don't see it."

For the most part, Rena was right. Very few churches have on their walls reproductions of great Christian art.

"But our faith tells us, 'The Word became flesh,'" Rena would say. That idea was hammered into my head time and time again. It was with a velvet hammer, however, for Rena never took a holier-than-thou attitude. Rather, in a kind way, she wanted to be sure that this young minister would understand the Word in its fuller meaning. A few years later, her artistic seeds produced fruit as I moved to my second parish, and one of the projects I undertook was to see that some good Christian art was displayed on the walls of the church.

One of the things I learned from Rena Hansen is how blind we can be without realizing it. When I returned to Yale Divinity School for some continuing education, I noticed on the walls of most of the classrooms there was great Christian art depicting various events in the Bible. I commented to the dean that it was good to see Christian art on the walls of the seminary and asked, "Did you get these recently?"

He looked at me kind of funny and said, "They were here when you were here."

Unfortunately, earlier I didn't get the Word. Rena Hansen changed that.

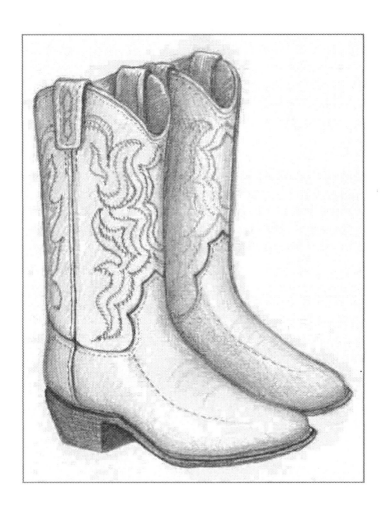

5

More than Cowboy Boots

"Boy, now that yur in Texas, we gotta git you some cowboy boots!"

With a thick but warm Texas accent—that's how John Hardie greeted me when I became minister of First Christian Church in Duncanville, Texas. Actually, I was born in Texas, but I had been to a lot of places since then, and the fact was: I didn't have any cowboy boots. John took care of that.

John Hardie's picture could have been on a brochure advertising Texas. He was almost a portrait of what the rest of the country thinks Texans look like. When he walked into a room, his stature commanded attention. He was a big man with a stomach that slightly hung over his big belt buckle. He had a large head of beautiful silver hair combed back on the sides. He wore a handsome Stetson hat and, of course, cowboy boots.

John was a strong Christian and a firm believer in tithing (giving ten percent of income to the church). In addition to his regular giving on Sunday, from time to time, he would sell some property or gain additional income in some way, and he would come to me and say, "Pastor, I've got some of the Lord's money. Do you have any special projects you need done?" That was like saying to a hungry man, "Do you want something to eat?"

Over the years, the church's ministry was enhanced by such projects as a new sound system in the sanctuary with listening devices for the hearing impaired, video equipment so we could tape the sermon for shut-ins, as well as make the worship service available on public access television. We also acquired a special Christian art project. This was comprised of reproductions of masterpieces of Christian art throughout the centuries. The paintings were framed and hung on the walls of the church, and I wrote a book about the paintings and artists. John and his wife, Catherine, underwrote the publication of the book and made it available for all members of the congregation. This was an excellent Christian education project.

John not only loved the church, but he also had a great respect for the clergy. Whenever the adult Sunday-school class went out to eat, he always insisted on picking up the check for the minister. I remember one time my wife and I were eating in a Mexican food restaurant. John and Catherine entered, saw us, and came over to say a friendly "Howdy" before they sat down. When the meal was over and I went to pay, the cashier said, "It has already been taken care of."

John was one of fifteen elders in the church, a lay ministry group. We had an elders' shepherding program in which each elder had a portion of the congregation in a "flock." In addition to hospital calls I would make, the elder took communion to members of the flock who were in the hospital. John suggested that the elders increase their ministry to church members in the hospital by making available the anointing of oil as it is outlined in the New Testament: "Are any among you sick? They should call for the elders of the church and have them pray over them, anointing them with oil in the name of the Lord." (James 5:14) This became a meaningful experience for many members of the church.

One day, John came to my study and announced that he was selling his house. He wanted to get away from the noise and bright lights of the city, and he planned to build a house in a wooded area a couple of miles out of town. He wanted me to come bless the property and the anticipated house. I wrote a small service and a prayer, and stood with John and Catherine on their property and asked God to bless the endeavor.

Shortly after the house was completed, God blessed the area in a way John hadn't particularly wanted. A megachurch bought the property across the road from his house, built a huge building, a school that was filled with noisy kids, and a large parking lot that was filled with bright lights. Many people might have felt hard toward God about that, but not John. His outlook on life was that things always happen for a reason, and that God has an ultimate purpose for each of our lives. He developed this outlook early. When he was in high school, he played baseball and played it very well. In fact, a scout for a farm team to one of the major leagues was interested in John. Then John developed polio and could no longer play baseball. He walked with a limp for the rest of his life.

As John told me the story, he said, "I was really disappointed at first, but I've come to realize that God had a different plan for my life. Maybe He realized that if I went to the major leagues I would be traveling a lot and that wouldn't work too well for a family. Family is really important."

Family was important to John, but concern for family meant not only the immediate family. John saw everyone as a child of God and therefore his brother or sister. If he saw someone who needed help, he responded to that person as family.

After John passed away, his son David continued the family's produce business. One day when David was out of town, his secretary received a phone call, which she relayed to him in the following note:

"David, I took a call today for you. This woman moved to Texas from New Mexico many years ago as a young woman. Her father was a preacher and he had a friend who knew your father.

"Before she left New Mexico, he gave her John Hardie's telephone number and told her that if she ever got in a bind, she could call him for help. Subsequently, after her arrival here, she lost her job and had no money, and actually did call your dad to ask for help. Without having ever met her before, your dad wrote her a check for $500 and told her to pay it back just whenever she could. She said that money, which was a fairly large sum at the time, enabled her to stay in her apartment and pay the bills until she found a job and got back on her feet. She then paid the money back.

"That all happened many years ago. The woman has a grown daughter now, but she called today to let you know that she has never forgotten the kindness of your father, and whenever she sees a Hardie's truck, she thinks fondly of him."

With a simple trusting faith and a generous heart, John Hardie had much more to offer than a pair of cowboy boots.

6

The Dirty Old Man

If you ever needed a hubcap for a 1939 Studebaker, Lee Collins probably had it in his garage. Lee collected and held on to everything "because I might need it some day." He did, in fact, make use of much of his stuff. When I first came to First Christian Church in Duncanville, Lee came into my small office, introduced himself, and in his slow, quiet voice asked, "You doin' all right? Can I fix anything for you?" I thanked him, but before I could think of anything, he noticed that the plastic cover to the small window in the office door didn't latch but just hung open.

"I'll be right back," he said with a smile. Lee retreated to his little pickup, rummaged through his stuff, and came up with some little gizmo that wasn't intended for a latch, but it worked.

Lee was always fixing things in the church, even though the fixing was often unorthodox. If anyone noticed some repair that looked a little strange, the comment was, "Oh, that's a 'Lee Collins special.'" However, even though Lee's fixings were often unconventional, everyone knew his intentions were good and he loved the church.

One day Lee discovered a local car dealership was getting rid of their outdoor sign. The sign was to be thrown away, but Lee managed to obtain it and planted it in the front of the church to advertise the times of the service.

Lee was married to Elizabeth Daniel, whose great grandparents, R.N. and Frances Daniel, were two of the key founders of the church in 1893. That made Lee a "patriarch-in-law," and everyone respected him as such. When I became minister, he had already been elected elder emeritus, which is the highest lay office in the church. This election made Lee a permanent member of the official board, which meets every month.

Board meetings are not my favorite part of the ministry. In my first church out of seminary where I served as associate minister, the senior minister always planned to take a long walk after each board meeting. I soon discovered why. Board meetings are necessary, I'm sure, but you never know what might happen. Someone could get upset about something and come to the board meeting to let off steam or fuss. Of course, if they were upset about something, I would rather know it than not know it. It's not good to let things fester. At the same time it was good to have levelheaded people like Lee Collins at the meetings. More than once in his mild and warm manner, he defused possible explosions.

Although Lee Collins was church royalty, to meet him for the first time you would never know it by his appearance. He often wore wrinkled work clothes as he drove up to the church in his several-year-old little pickup with his dog, Lucy, sitting next to him. The story goes that Lee came up to the church in the middle of the week to ask the minister if he needed anything fixed at the church. The minister was standing in the parking lot talking to someone who wanted information about the church. As Lee walked up, the man commented to the minister, "Who's this dirty old man?" Although probably said in jest, the minister thought it was inappropriate, but Lee got a kick out of it. He never tired of telling the story, and often referred to himself as "the dirty old man."

I once found and sent Lee a birthday card that had "Happy Birthday" on the front, and when you opened the card, there was a little bar of soap with the caption, "Dirty old men need love, too." I am not sure Elizabeth appreciated it, but Lee loved it.

7

The Man of Many Talents

Some people spend a lifetime in one vocation. Jim Buckner had several. He had been a fighter pilot in World War II. He flew the airplanes that I made models of when I was a boy...P-40 Kitty Hawk, P-51 Mustang, and the twin tailed P-38 Lightning. I could sit all day and listen to stories he would tell. Not only did he fly fighter planes, but later he was connected with the Organization of American States, where he was called on from time to time to fly in and defuse potential revolutions. Then he was in charge of future projects and the pilots connected with them, one of whom was a man by the name of Neil Armstrong.

After World War II, Jim became a ski instructor, and he told me of a conversation he had with Jean-Claude Killy who later won three skiing gold medals in the 1968 Winter Olympics. Then Jim took up motorcycles. Some time after that he decided to enter a chiropractic college. At the age of fifty-two Jim graduated with a doctor's degree and began another vocation. He was practicing this vocation when he became a member of First Christian Church.

One Sunday soon after he and his wife, Annell, joined, I twisted my back on the way to the church. Jim went through the line at the end of the worship service and said, "You seem to be moving slowly. Did you hurt your back?" I told him what happened and he replied, "Follow me to my office, and I'll fix you up."

I had never been to a chiropractor before, and I had heard all kinds of stories of why to stay away from them. Jim must have sensed my hesitation, for he asked, "Have you ever been to a chiropractor?" When I shook my head, he grinned and said, "There is a lot of misinformation about chiropractors. We're not really 'quacks' like some people think. I promise not to hurt you…and the first time I won't even bring out the snakes."

I figured someone with such a sense of humor couldn't be all that bad, so I followed Jim to his office where he did indeed fix me up. The fact that he wouldn't take anything for his services made it even better.

Jim is the kind of person who really wants to help people…and not only people. One day Jim heard about a church member's dog that had been injured in an accident and was in pain. Jim said, "Let me see the dog." He adjusted the dog's back, and the dog stopped whimpering and began to lick his hand.

Jim cares not only for the physical concerns of people, but he also spreads emotional joy. Jim is a hugger. He is always hugging people in the church. People are drawn to him as a warm, caring person and as a leader. He has held several leadership positions, including chair of the official board and chair of the elders…the elders being the highest spiritual lay office in the church.

As I write this, Jim is in his eighties, but you wouldn't know it to see him. Although a decade and a half older than I, he has twice as much energy and three times as much hair. When I ask him when he is going to slow down, he grins and says, "Not until I decide what I'm going to do when I grow up."

8

The Computer Angel

When I began my ministry, the office equipment in the first church I served consisted of a telephone, a manual typewriter, and a mimeograph machine. Over the course of my ministry, technology mushroomed as telephones advanced to include answering machines and phone trees with the capability of sending messages to everyone in the congregation. The mimeograph has been replaced by the copier, and the typewriter has given way to the computer. All this has enhanced the capability of ministry, but with every blessing comes a challenge.

Let me illustrate with a bit of personal history. When I graduated from high school and headed to college, my parents gave me a portable manual typewriter. That typewriter saw me through paper after paper during four years of college, four years of seminary, and several years of graduate school, all amounting to four academic degrees. That typewriter still works as well today as the day my parents gave it to me, although now it sits lonely in a closet, because now I have a computer.

I held off buying a computer for a long time. When computers for the ordinary guy became popular, I remember someone my age said to me, "Why don't you get a computer?"

"What would I use it for?" I asked.

"Well, you could make a list on the computer of what you need at the grocery store and then print it out."

"Why couldn't I just write the list on a piece of paper?"

He didn't answer. As I said, he was my age, and I'm sure he felt getting a computer was the avant-garde thing to do, even if he wasn't completely sure what to do with it. Younger people, of course, don't have that problem. Whereas my generation grew up with typewriters, they grew up with computers and never questioned them. That's just the way the world was.

As I said, I held out for a long time, but a turning point came one day when I went to the public library. Not only did I grow up with the typewriter, but I also grew up with the card-catalog system in the library. Then all of a sudden, there was no card catalog, just a computer. I couldn't even find an on-off switch.

I have to admit now, even though I didn't admit it at the time, I was scared of computers. Then I heard that when Benjamin Harrison was president of the United States, electricity was added to the White House, and he was scared of it but didn't want to admit it. In the evening when it started to get dark, he would wait until someone came in the room, and he would casually say, "Oh, since you're standing by the light switch, would you please turn it on?" I don't know what he did if no one came in—sat in the dark, I suppose.

Not wanting to sit in the dark, I gave in to technology and bought a computer. I learned how to turn it on (although I still don't know why they don't have a switch labeled "on-off"). But then I quickly found myself in the dark. I asked my teen-age son, Ryan, who grew up with computers in school, "What do I do now?"

He said, "Oh that's easy," and he punched a few keys, "or you could do it this way," and he punched a few more keys, "or you could do it this way."

"Wait a minute!" I screamed. "I don't need to know three ways, only one."

It was at this point that I decided I needed to take a computer class, and I needed to have it taught by someone my age, who did not grow up with computers and who could understand my stupid questions. That was several years ago, and I have come to appreciate the computer and realize it can be used for more than just making grocery lists. I would hate to have to type the manuscript for this book on my old manual typewriter, even though it still works.

To get back to a statement I made earlier: "With every blessing comes a challenge." Computers in many ways are a blessing, but unlike my manual typewriter, which has lasted decades, computers need to be replaced about every three or four years, and even during those three or four years there is always something wrong with them. At first, I thought it was just my computer, that I got a lemon or something. But then I discovered time and time again, as I was talking on the phone to a bank teller or someone in a business, and the person at the other end would hesitate and then say, "I'm sorry, the computer is down" or "I'm sorry, the computers are very slow today."

This long introduction leads up to the personality in the pew for this chapter, and that is the computer angel. Since computers are always acting up (even those computers in the church that are doing the Lord's work), everyone needs a computer angel. One of the computer angels at First Christian Church was Bill Faulkner. Bill was very talented with computers, and he was very generous with his talents. He was a computer guardian angel hovering in the wings of the church, ready to swoop down and do battle with computer demons. When something in the computer wasn't working right, I would think, *This is probably a simple thing. Bill will know what to do.* And Bill always did know what to do, but seldom was it simple...at least it wasn't simple to me.

On one occasion when the phone call didn't provide enough therapy for the computer, I had to take it to Bill's home for surgery. Bill greeted me at the door, and he escorted me into the computer inner sanctum, a special room in the house dedicated to computers. There, built into the wall was a beautiful wood cabinet with two state-of-the-art computers, each with two large monitors, one for Bill and one for his wife

Deb. Two very elegant and comfortable chairs sat behind each computer. There were also various electronic equipment pieces all around the room. The room was warmer than the rest of the house, and Bill commented that they had already added special air conditioning dedicated to the room, but with all the heat from the computers and equipment, the air conditioner couldn't quite keep up. I left the sick computer with the good doctor, and in a few days, he called to say it was fixed, and I was back in the cyberspace business.

As I said before, computers are a blessing. Our church newsletter looked much more professional and creative than it did in the days before the computer. With the computer, we could better keep up with church members' addresses and phone numbers. There were all kinds of things we could do better with the computer, but as I also said before, with this blessing comes a challenge. There are days when the computer demons will bring dark clouds of frustration and cause a minister to utter words that should never be heard in public. But, with a computer angel like Bill Faulkner, the demons can be routed, for the moment at least, and the sun will break through the clouds allowing ministry to continue.

9

A Shiny Red Suit and a Song

Luther Langford had a heart as big as the state of Texas. In addition to his big heart, he had a technical mind. He was an electrician, which was good for the church because if any electrical work was needed, he did it for free.

Luther also loved kids, and one year the church asked him to play the part of Santa Claus for the church Christmas party, so he rented a Santa suit and gave away Christmas candy to all the kids in the church. He enjoyed it so much he decided to do it every year. He went to a seamstress and had a Santa suit made out of shiny red satin, which was much more elegant than any rented suit. The only trouble was, Luther had the suit made to fit him perfectly without any padding, and Luther was much higher than he was wide. This was good for his heart but not so good for impersonating a plump Santa. Luther also had a distinctive voice, which made it difficult to conceal his identity. But he loved playing the part, and every year as the highlight of the church Christmas party, a tall lanky Santa with a very shiny form-fitting red suit would make his entrance, and with a thick Texas accent, he would shout, "Merry Christmas, boys and girls!" He would then sit in a big chair while all the kids lined up to sit on his lap, tell Santa what they wanted for Christmas, and then receive a bag of Christmas candy. The first time our daughter, Angela, sat on his lap, she had a troubled look on her face, and afterward announced she didn't think that was really Santa. It was "just Luther."

This reminded me of my first experience with a questionable Santa, when I was a very young boy. It was at a Woolworth five-and-dime store in McAllen, Texas. Unlike Luther, this Santa was plump enough, but Santa's voice was unmistakably female. When I announced to my parents that this couldn't be Santa, my mother explained that the real Santa was very busy at Christmas time and couldn't be everywhere, and this lady was one of Santa's helpers. That explanation worked for me, so we tried it with Angela. Apparently, it worked for her, for without any further questioning, she went straight to opening her bag of Christmas candy. There may have been other children with similar questions, but then that was for their parents to deal with.

Angela had been exposed to Luther's voice more than most of the other kids in the church. Luther and his wife, Frances, were some of her first babysitters. Angela was a toddler at the time, and my wife and I took her to their home while we set out for a dinner sans child. When we returned, we found Luther on the floor playing with Angela, and with a big grin, he informed us that he had taught her how to untie her shoes.

Frances Langford loved children as much as Luther did. In fact, she became known to everyone in the church as Granny Frances. She taught Sunday school and Vacation Church School. She loved to teach the children new songs, and they loved to hug her neck.

If Luther had a heart as large as the state of Texas, Frances had a faith that was that large. She was often asked to lead the worship for the Christian Women's Fellowship. Her faith was outgoing, and it was deeply personal.

One day, after Frances had a series of chest pains and shortness of breath, the doctor discovered she had a severe blockage in one of her arteries. He told her he would attempt angioplasty, but if it didn't work, it would require bypass surgery. Frances said to the doctor, "I sincerely hope the angioplasty will work. I know bypass surgery takes a long time to heal, and I can't be away from church that long."

During the procedure, the doctor tried several times to insert the balloon in the artery, but each time it was unsuccessful. Frances was awake during this process, and the doctor finally informed her that the angioplasty wasn't working.

"Try one more time," Frances pleaded.

"But Frances, I tried several times, and it just won't work," the doctor replied.

Frances repeated, "Try one more time. I'm praying really hard this time."

The doctor tried one more time…and it worked.

Luther and Frances were unique. Although they have been gone for several years as I write this, their memory is still strong in the church. When I think of them in heaven, I can see Luther in his shiny red suit playing Santa for all the angels' kids, and Granny Frances teaching them to sing some new song in heaven's Vacation Church School.

10

The Extended Pew

Some of the personalities, who are the most dedicated to the church, don't sit in the pews that reside in the sanctuary. I'm referring to those people who once occupied church pews every week but now, because of age or poor health, can no longer do so. They are often referred to as shut-ins or as the home bound, and I have found that getting to know some of these personalities in the extended pew has been a sheer delight.

A Teacher for More Than Four Decades

Mildred Matney began teaching school in 1934, when she was eighteen years old. She taught for forty-two years. Once, when I visited her in the nursing home, I asked about her experiences as a teacher.

She immediately began reminiscing: "I taught mainly in country schools…in places with names like Buffalo Springs and Antelope. Sometimes I had to take off my shoes and stockings and wade across some water to get to school. In my first school, two of the boys were older than I was, but I never had any trouble with them. One of the boys I knew already, because he lived on the next country road. He called me Minke…short for McKinney, I guess, which was my maiden name. I took him off in the corner and said, 'You can call me Minke outside of class, but here call me Miss McKinney.'

"'OK,' he said.

"During the war all the men teachers were called to war, and the head of the school board came to me and said, 'We need a superintendent until another man comes.'

"I said, 'Oh.'

"He said, 'Guess what? It's you.'

"That was very unusual for women to be superintendents in those days. So, I had the responsibility of being in charge, and those country boys were really a rowdy bunch. They liked to do things like turn the outhouses upside down. But I got the older boys in a group and told them, 'Now you know all our men teachers are gone to war, and we all have to do our part. Will you help me keep the younger boys in line?'

"They said, 'OK,' and I never had any problems."

After awhile Mrs. Matney paused and said, "But I'm boring you with all my personal stories. You've got more important things to do than to listen to my ramblings."

I wasn't bored at all. Her quiet reminiscing transported me back to an earlier time, and reminded me of stories my father told about growing up in Arkansas where he attended a one-room schoolhouse...perhaps like the one in which Mrs. Matney taught.

When I visited Mrs. Matney, she always thanked me for coming and acted as if I had performed a great ministry by my presence, but in reality, I always left feeling I was the one who had been ministered to.

An Unsolicited Reward

T.W. Hooper had several strokes and was confined to his home, which incidentally was one of the nicest homes in the congregation. He had been owner and manager of the local Ford dealership and had been quite good at it. In fact, he was so good at establishing and getting dealerships off the ground, Ford sent him all over the country to do just that. He finally sold his dealership and retired, but soon after that, he found himself to be a shut-in and unable to come to church.

Whenever I visited, he asked about the church and showed a genuine interest, but then the conversation eventually went to his experiences in World War II. He said, "At various times I was in several branches of the service...the Army, the Navy, and the Air Force," and then he would go into detail how all this came about. I heard these stories time and time again, but somehow he managed to make them fresh and interesting with each retelling. Except for a prayer at the end of the visit, my calls mainly consisted of listening to his stories. On one of my visits, without fanfare or any self-congratulations, he calmly handed me a check made out to the church for fifty thousand dollars.

A Happy Camper

Verba Blevins had been active in the church for years, but by the time I came to Duncanville, she was in a nursing home. The first time I visited her she acted as though she had known me for years. I then discovered from the head nurse that she had dementia and didn't really remember anyone in her family, or anyone else who visited. The remarkable thing was how pleasant and positive she was. While others in the nursing home complained much of the time, or just sat there and said or did nothing, she was a bundle of joy and full of conversation.

"How are you today, Mrs. Blevins?" I asked.

"I'm just great," she would reply. "I just got back from milking the cows, and the cows are doing just fine."

Then she would tell me all the visitors she had had that day (some of whom had died several years ago) and how they were all doing fine. Often she would interrupt herself to warn me, "Be careful of those cats. Don't rock on their tails." The fact that there were no cats and that I wasn't sitting in a rocker didn't seem to matter to her. She would then be off on sharing with me some other ventures or introducing me to her roommate, the name of whom she changed every time I came. At the end of my visit, I had a prayer with her, which she thanked me for. I told her I would be back to see her, and she thanked me again.

Because of the unreality of her conversation, I know that the head nurse must have been right about her condition, but I couldn't help but feel that somewhere down deep inside, she was responding to the good experiences and warmth she had felt when she was sitting in the pews of the church. Because of these good experiences, now in the extended pew she chose to be positive and happy, and this was indeed a blessing for her and for everyone around her.

11

The Rumble-seat Pew

I have always had an interest in cars, and I see them as much more than mere transportation. I remember in high school my dad and I overhauled a 1950 Studebaker. We ground the valves, planed the head, and put in oversized pistons. That model Studebaker was so underpowered that even our modifications only meant I could out-drag other 1950 Studebakers, but it was still fun.

Two Blue Porsches

In 1958, I spent one of my seminary years as an exchange student from Yale to the University of Edinburgh in Scotland, and one of the American exchange students there bought a new Porsche Speedster. It was much less expensive to buy it over there because there was no special high tax, as long as the person took the car out of the country within the year. However, this student decided he wanted to stay another year in school, so he was looking for someone who was leaving at the end of the year to buy it, so he wouldn't have to pay the tax. I phoned my parents in Seattle, Washington, who checked with a bank. Because of the low price of the car, we figured I could borrow the money from the bank, drive the car from New York to

Seattle, and sell it for what I paid for it before returning to seminary, which meant I could drive around all summer in a Porsche. For a twenty-three-year-old seminary student, what a deal! I made arrangements to return to the United States on a cargo freighter leaving out of Liverpool. The student selling the car was to meet me at the dock with the car. On the way to Liverpool, he wrecked the car! The student wasn't hurt, but the car was totaled. So ended my nirvana summer.

A few years later, when I served as associate minister in Warren, Ohio, I had the opportunity to buy a used Porsche Speedster convertible exactly the same color as the one in Edinburgh. However, this experience too ended in tragedy. Traveling with my friend, Fred Harris, on a back road in Pennsylvania, we hit an oil slick and spun out. With the top down, the car turned over and landed straddling a ditch. With our seat belts on, we were hanging upside down with our heads in the space of the ditch. Had the car not landed that way, we would have been decapitated. I can remember seeing the sunset that evening and realizing how grateful I was to be alive, how precious and fragile life is, and how perhaps God had saved me for some important purpose. I also felt like God was telling me to get out of the sports-car driving business.

A Milder Car

After the Porsche incident, my interest in cars took a turn in another direction. Several years later, I was driving by a used car lot in Duncanville, Texas, and I saw this beautiful yellow and black 1929 Model A Roadster. I thought it was there as a "come-on" to get people to stop and look at the other cars, but the smiling salesman said, "It's for sale. Take it for a spin." I took it home. My wife, Gloria, and our four-year-old daughter, Angela, got in the rumble seat. We strapped our six-month-old son, Ryan, in a car seat next to me, and we drove all over town with everyone we saw smiling and giving us a thumbs-up. I was hooked and bought the car.

In the next nineteen years, the Model A became a part of the ministry of the church. I made all my pastoral calls in it. When I made evangelism calls, I made a hit with the kids, who always wanted to sit in the rumble seat and hear the "ooga" horn. When I went to the grocery store, people were always coming up to me in the parking lot to see the car, which gave me the opportunity to tell them I was the minister at First Christian Church and invite them to church if they didn't already have a church home. I also advertised the church by driving the car in several Fourth of July parades.

The Model A always drew comments. The kids all over town were constantly yelling, "Honk your horn!" The next most-yelled comment was, "What year is it?" When I called back "'29," one kid looked a little puzzled and asked, "1929 or 1829?"

However, kids were not the only ones to call out comments. On one occasion, I was sitting at a stoplight, and the president of the bank pulled up beside me in his new Cadillac. He looked over at me, rolled down his window, and said, "You look like you're having more fun than anybody."

The rumble seat of the Model A became a favorite for brides and grooms to leave in after the wedding ceremony. The most popular use of the rumble seat, however, came at Christmastime. I drew up a driving route to the homes of all our shut-ins, and members of the church went in a car caravan to each house to sing Christmas carols. The kids in the church took turns riding in the rumble seat as we drove from house to house. I even made numbered tickets to give out, so everyone would get a chance to ride. One year when the weather was bad and it was raining, I expected the kids to opt for riding in one of the other cars since the rumble seat was open to the elements, but they still lined up for tickets for the Model A. There was always as much singing on the road as there was in front of the houses, intermittent with calls from the rumble seat to "Honk the horn!"

On one occasion, we were at a stoplight, and a Corvette pulled up beside us. A teenager was driving (probably his dad's car) with his date sitting next to him. She looked over while the kids in the rumble seat were singing at the top of their lungs, "Rudolph the Red-Nosed Reindeer."

She rolled down the window and said, "Want to trade cars?"

I smiled and said, "No thanks."

Of all the cars I have owned, the Model A has been the friendliest. It brought back memories for the older people, questions for the not so old, "Honk your horn" for the kids, and smiles for everyone. At my retirement party at the church, several adults shared with me that one of their fondest memories of growing up in the church was riding in the rumble seat and caroling shut-ins at Christmas. The rumble seat truly became an important pew in the church.

12

The Sweet Sister Gambit

One of my concerns when I came to First Christian Church in Duncanville was the address of the church. The church faced Avenue C, so the address was 206 South Avenue C. The problem was that there was no Avenue A, nor Avenue B, so when the newspaper listed our address, no one knew where we were. It was doubly frustrating because although the back of the church faced Main Street (a street everyone would know), there was a vacant lot between us and Main, and the post office wouldn't let us use a Main Street address. If, however, we could purchase the vacant lot, we could accomplish two tasks: build on the lot to expand the church and get a Main Street address.

When we looked into purchasing the vacant lot, we were told it was owned by two elderly sisters who apparently had had a quarrel some years back. The story was that each thought she was right. They weren't even speaking to one another, and the property was tied up in court. This meant that our project was put on hold while hoping for reconciliation between the sisters or a settlement in the court. For several years, neither option came to pass, but then something else did come to pass: one of the sisters passed away. Either to show up the other sister or out of pure generosity (I hope it was the latter), the sister who died willed her interest in the property to the church. Either not to be shown up by her sister or out of pure generosity (again, I hope it was the latter), the remaining sister donated her share to the church as well.

If there is a moral to this story, it might be "It is better to be good than right." At any rate, this closed the door to the feud and opened the door to the post office for a new church address as soon as we finished our building project, and that is the subject of the next chapter.

203

13

The Main Event

First: Study

Bob Daniel could remember Duncanville when you identified houses not by street and numbers, but simply by the names of the people who lived there. By the time I came to Duncanville in 1976, it was a fast-growing suburb of Dallas, but Bob, who lived right behind me and shared an alley, loved to cross the alley and tell me stories of early Duncanville. Bob's grandparents, R.N. and Frances Daniel, were two of the main founders of the church in 1893. His parents were also key church leaders, so Bob's respected name, his easygoing manner, and his love for the church made him the perfect choice for chair of the Building Study Committee.

Being the chair of this committee was not an easy job. Bob had to listen to everyone who had a pet project, as well as listen to those who were sure they knew exactly what should and should not be built. He had to be aware of mothers with babies who were concerned about a bigger and better nursery, parents of teenagers who lobbied for a gym for the youth, and the cooking ladies who wanted a new stainless-steel kitchen. He also had to balance needs with what the church could afford. Bob patiently listened to everyone, thanked them for their input, and assured them that he would share their concerns with the whole committee.

The committee completed its study and worked up a proposal, which included more Sunday-school classrooms, new offices, a better nursery, a combination gym/fellowship hall, a remodeled sanctuary, and the ladies got their stainless-steel kitchen. Bob made the presentation to the Official Board. After some discussion, the board passed the proposal unanimously. It then went to the congregation, which also passed it. Generally, there was great excitement about the new venture, which was now passed on to two other committees: the Building Fund Committee to raise the money and the Building Committee to oversee the construction.

Next: Get the Money

John Detmore had a strong opinion about everything, and he generously shared it. However, he was a go-getter, and he loved the church, so he was asked to chair the Building Fund Committee. The total for the Study Committee's proposal added up to close to a million dollars. We called in the experts to help us with raising the money, and their initial response was that a church our size probably could not raise that much. John responded, "You're wrong!" (in a little stronger language). Then he added, "We can do it!"

The experts shrugged and said, "OK, try it," and they gave us a manual suggesting how to organize a fundraising campaign.

The campaign was a comprehensive program, with several subcommittees to handle publicity, letter writing, articles for the newsletter, pleas from the pulpit, and personal calling on the members. On the first night when these subcommittees were meeting at various homes in the congregation, John wanted to make an appearance at every meeting in order to give a pep talk. I had just purchased a 1929 Model A Roadster, and I took every opportunity to be in it, so I offered to drive. It was a nice evening, so I put the top down, and we tootled from place to place. As we drove, I noticed John kept one hand placed firmly on the top of his head. That was the night I discovered that John wore a toupee.

We set out to get three-year pledges from everyone in the congregation, so we could use them as collateral to borrow the money. On the first Sunday that we made an appeal, after the service, John came running up to me, wide eyed, almost dancing a jig, and waving a piece of paper. It was a check. Hattie Mae Hoskins, without any fanfare, had simply dropped a check in the offering plate for one hundred thousand dollars. The campaign was off to a good start. The building could now commence.

Finally: Build

Ray Dean was an engineer during the week, but on Sunday, he was the church sidewalk sweeper. It wasn't a paid position, nor was it a responsibility connected with any committee he was on. He simply took it upon himself to make sure people coming to church had a pristinely clean cement path on their way to worship. Ray's engineering talents, his ability to see things that needed to be done, and his love for the church made him the perfect choice for chair of the Building Committee.

For the most part, things went smoothly in this committee, but there were a couple of bumps along the road. It is interesting how often the big things are agreed upon without a hitch, while some small issue causes some ruffled feathers. Such was the case in choosing the color for repainting the sanctuary. The last time the sanctuary was repainted, it was paid for by one of the committee members whose wife chose the color. It just so happened that this committee member was out of town when the committee chose the color to repaint this time, and since it was not the color his wife had previously chosen, he claimed the committee waited until he was not there to pick the color. It was my job as pastor to try to smooth out ruffled feathers.

(When we all get to heaven, I want to be sure I'm not on the committee deciding what color to repaint the Pearly Gates.)

An important step was to get a general contractor. Don Cutler was an outgoing person with a keen sense of humor and a pleasing personality. He had gone to a conservative religious college, and some of the people there tried to convince him to go into the ministry. But rather than working to build the Kingdom, he decided to become a contractor and work to build houses. This was a benefit to the Kingdom, however, since he offered his services to the church at no cost for this project.

The next several months involved many meetings with Don Cutler. I remember one meeting at our home with blueprints and samples spread out all over the kitchen table. Angela, our young daughter, liked Don, but she was a little shy. She sat at the table across from Don, and without saying a word, she rolled one of her cookies toward him. Don looked up, and with a broad smile said, "Roll-y things!" Our daughter is now an adult, but to her, those particular cookies are still "roll-y things."

Don took a personal interest in making the new building "just right." The combination gym/fellowship hall functioned as a gym with special gym carpet, but Don's design made it look like a fellowship hall. He installed bright lights for sports, but he said, "These lights will make your food look purple, so I'm going to install another set to be used for dinners."

As far as offices were concerned, Don not only designed an attractive and functional main office, but he also had said to me from the beginning, "If I don't do anything else, I'm going to make you a nice office." My office I think had originally been a big closet. It was right next to the sanctuary, and when the organ was playing during choir practice, you couldn't hear yourself think, and the vibrations caused things to bounce up and down on my desk. A window air conditioner made so much noise that I had to turn it off during counseling sessions. In addition to all this, the door was paper thin, and anyone passing by could hear the conversation or counseling going on inside.

True to his word, Don made a beautiful (and soundproof) minister's study in the new building.

Another person who was directly involved in this whole process was Bobby Cutler, Don's wife. Bobby was a petite woman, always immaculately dressed, and she had a talent for interior decorating. I have never seen a minister's study as beautiful as the one she designed.

Once the new building was completed, the sanctuary remodeling began. Since this involved scaffolding to take the 1950s acoustic tile off the ceiling and replace it with wood, the operation took several weeks. We held worship services in the new gym/fellowship hall. We couldn't move the organ to the fellowship hall, but even if we could have, that organ was an old electronic one, which was not much better than a keyboard. I managed to get a state-of-the-art organ on loan to be set up in the fellowship hall, with the hope someone would say, "Let's get it." My hope bore fruit as Hattie Mae Hoskins came to me after the first service in the fellowship hall and asked, "Would it be possible to have that organ in the sanctuary?"

"Yes, ma'am," I replied, smiling, as she wrote out a check.

September 24, 1989, found the building project completed with a processional from the fellowship hall to the sanctuary, led by the bell choir. There was just one more event to take place—a trip to the post office to change the address from Avenue C to Main Street. They gave me the opportunity to choose 201, 203, or 207. With years of trying to bring together those on the theological right and those on the theological left, I chose the middle number, and the church address became 203 South Main Street.

14

Responses to Preaching

"Pastor, that was absolutely the worst sermon I have ever heard."

This was the statement made to me by one of the patients at Elgin State Mental Hospital where I served as a chaplain intern during my seminary training. There were several of us who took turns preaching to the geriatric ward once a week, and this was the response made to me as this patient went through the line after the sermon. Catching my breath, I managed to say something like, "Well, I'm glad at least you listened."

The next week I was scheduled to preach to that ward again. After the sermon, the same patient came through the line and said, "Well, Pastor, I didn't think you could do it." He paused, then continued, "But this sermon was worse than the last." Then he laughed. I found out later to my relief that he made that statement to every new student chaplain who preached. However, there were many other situations where patients went through the line after the sermon and responded not in a joking way, but responded with exactly what was on their minds. This was the norm rather than the exception.

My experience of people's responses to a sermon in the local church is much different from what I experienced in the mental hospital. However, before I say more about that, let me say that most people are not aware of what a minister does with his time...especially in the area of sermon preparation. Yet I suppose that is true of many professions. I once asked a commercial artist in my church if he would make a poster to put on the bulletin board to advertise a Bible study. I figured he could do it in half an hour or so. I later discovered he spent five hours working on it. The same situation is true for sermon preparation. In seminary I was taught that a good sermon requires one hour of preparation for every minute preached, which means that for a twenty-minute sermon there are twenty hours of preparation. I shared this with one of the personalities in the pews, and he was dumbfounded. "I just thought you got up there and preached," he said. Then he added, "But knowing now all the time you put into preparation, I'm going to pay more attention."

I am convinced, however, that a preacher rarely knows how the personalities in the pews are affected by a sermon. Unlike my experience of responses in the mental hospital, people in the local church usually go through the line saying something like, "That was a wonderful message," or "I really enjoyed your sermon," more often than not with the same casual tone of voice as you would say, "How are you today?" It's not that I believe reactions to sermons are casual or unimportant. My theory about preaching is that a preacher must do a thorough Bible study, prepare the very best sermon possible, deliver the sermon from the pulpit with conviction, and then let God use it to touch the hearts of those who hear. But rarely will the preacher see the results as the people go through the greeting line at the end of the sermon.

There are exceptions to this. When preaching hits a nerve, sometimes there is a genuine response. I once preached on Paul's scripture "Be angry but do not sin" (Ephesians 4:26). Part of the message was that anger is a natural reaction, that we all get angry, and it is important to acknowledge this to ourselves so that we can deal with the anger. Going through the line after the service, one person said in a very loud and angry voice, "I want you to know I am a Christian, and I don't get angry!" I made a mental note to make a pastoral call.

Another time I was preaching on the first Sunday in Lent about the importance of acknowledging our sins and making our confession to God, which is a large part of what Lent is all about. I also announced that we were going to add the General Confession to the worship during the season of Lent. A parishioner came through the line, obviously agitated, and said, "I don't like the General Confession in the service. I live my life the best I can. I don't think I'm that bad." I made another mental note to make a pastoral call. It turned out he did feel he was that bad, and the encounter resulted in several counseling sessions.

So, I believe sermons are important and can make a difference in the lives of the personalities in the pews, but rarely does the preacher get a reflective or considered response as people go through the line at the end of the worship service. Maybe the mental hospital responses would be more helpful. It certainly would be more honest, and, possibly, it could open doors to genuine communication.

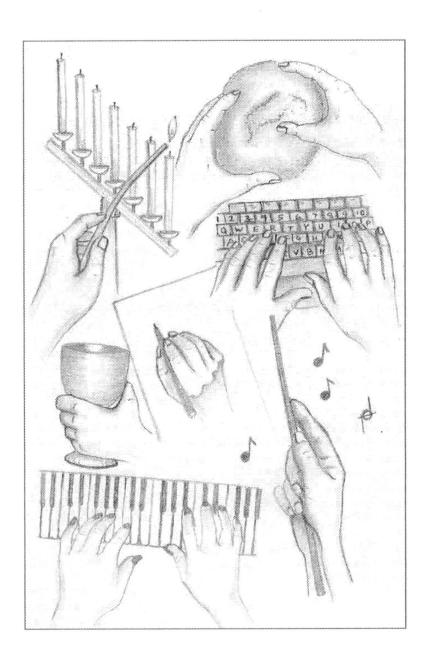

15

The Worshiping Pew

It's 10:45, and everything begins...but not really. It began long before that, although most people don't think about it. They simply walk into the sanctuary, get a worship bulletin, find a pew, perhaps smile at the person next to them, open a hymnbook, and expect the service to begin. Their expectations come true, but not before a lot of preparation took place.

In the last chapter, I said sermons are important, and I mentioned all the preparation that goes into a sermon, but there is even more preparation that goes into a worship service.

To begin with, that worship bulletin the worshiper gets requires a lot of preparation. The hymns have to be picked, as well as the Scripture and sermon title. This and any announcements have to get to the church secretary in time to prepare the bulletin. This may involve wrestling with the office equipment to be sure everything is done on time.

Other preparation involves the choir. Our choir at the church in Duncanville met on Wednesday evening every week, and sometimes more often if there was a special service coming up. The choir involved many personalities in the pews—in this case, the choir pews. It also involved a choir director. For years, in Duncanville, we had music students from Southern Methodist University as our choir directors. This was a win-win situation, since this gave the students some practical experience, and it gave us the enthusiasm of youth. After the church grew, we were able to hire a more permanent choir director—Jaime Perez, who taught music in the Dallas school system. Jamie brought a lot to the choir and therefore to the worship of the church. He provided a balance of classical, contemporary, and gospel music, so everyone could be musically fed. He also encouraged young people in the congregation to be a part of the worship service, and he often brought some of his students to perform.

The choir program also includes the bell choir, which practices every week, and the children's choir. Both are frequently a part of the worship service.

Connected with the choirs, but also more than that, is the organist. In the next chapter I will write more about the personalities involved in the organ pew, but here let me simply point out how important the organ is to worship and how much preparation is involved. My first office in the Duncanville church was next to the organ, and I can attest to the fact that the organist practiced frequently.

In the Christian Church (Disciples of Christ), we have Holy Communion every Sunday. This means some people have to prepare it beforehand and place the communion trays in the refrigerator, some people have to take the trays out of the refrigerator just before the service and put them on the communion table, and some people have to pass the communion trays during the service. Again, most worshipers sitting in the pews don't think about this, but if one of these links is left out, and during the service the minister moves from the lectern to the communion table and the communion trays are not there, suddenly everyone notices. This only happened to me once, but, fortunately, I noticed the missing communion trays early in the service, and with a quick note to a deacon and some scrambling in the kitchen, the trays appeared and worship continued.

The communion preparation is complicated by the fact that someone in the congregation bakes the communion bread. Cindy Bingham did this for years, and she felt this was an important part of worship. She told me she always said a prayer before she prepared the bread. She baked a dozen loaves at a time and placed them in the church freezer. Someone then had to take a loaf out of the freezer the night before the service, so it could thaw. Again, if this task was forgotten, and during the communion service, the minister held up the bread and attempted to break it, he would need an axe or a hacksaw. Fortunately, this never happened.

Other preparation involves scheduling deacons, elders, greeters, acolytes, and ushers: all of which are probably taken for granted by most worshipers, but would be sorely missed if they were not there. This applies also to the people working the audio system who turn on and adjust the microphones. Then there are the people who change the pulpit, lectern, and altar hangings to match the seasons of the church year, plus those who put flowers in the chancel. And don't forget the people who come early on Sunday morning to open the church and turn on the heat in the winter and the air conditioning in the summer. Even before that, there are the people who clean the sanctuary, and ready it for worship. In some churches, this is done by paid staff; in others, the parishioners do it. In either case, "cleanliness is next to godliness."

All of this is to point out how many people are involved and how much preparation there is for a worship service. And all of this is compounded when it comes to extra services in which all preparation has to start from scratch.

The main point I want to make, however, is that worship is very important and worthy of all the preparation. Worship can point us to that which is greater than ourselves and help us find meaning and purpose in life. Worship invites us to a relationship with an almighty and all-loving God. I believe that God has created us with a need to worship, and we are not complete unless this need is continually fulfilled. With that said, all I can add is, "Amen."

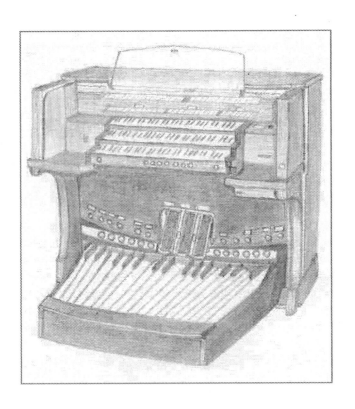

16

The Organ Pew

Good and Sweet

Her name was Nada, but no one called her that or even knew her name for that matter. Everyone called her Honey Bea. I never found out how she got the nickname, but it was appropriate, for she was a sweet person. However, it did cause some eyebrows raised at times. Honey Bea was the organist at the church, and if we were having a wedding rehearsal with someone who was not a member of the church or who didn't know her, I might say, "Honey Bea, would you play that introduction to the wedding march now," and people would wonder what our relationship was. She was too old to be my wife and too young to be my mother.

Honey Bea was sweet in more than one way. Not only did she have a kind and pleasant attitude, but she also had a dream that befitted her name. For years, she saved the money she received from the part-time organist position, and one day she came to me with her dream. She wanted to set up a scholarship fund for what she called "Music for Tomorrow." She wanted to encourage the young or even the not so young in the congregation to develop an interest in music. Her saved money was to remain as principal in a special account, and interest each year was to be awarded to whomever the Scholarship Committee might select. A plaque was erected and placed in the hall to honor the recipients. Over the years, the scholarship encouraged many people to develop their talents, and many Sundays found young people singing or playing a musical instrument in church during the worship service.

Honey Bea's Christian faith translated not only in her providing organ music for the worship service and scholarships for the music of tomorrow, but her faith also reflected in her work and daily life. She was a grade-school teacher, and she loved children. She especially cared about those who were underprivileged or had a difficult time in school. She learned Spanish so she could better communicate with her Hispanic students who had difficulty with English, and she learned signing so she could help those who had trouble hearing. She never gave up on anyone. There was a particular student who was withdrawn. He wouldn't try to learn; he wouldn't respond; he just sat in the back of the room. To all the other teachers he seemed incorrigible, and no one wanted him in his or her class. Honey Bea requested that they assign him to her class so she could work with him and give him special attention.

"He was really a smart kid," reflected Honey Bea. "He wasn't lost. He was just hidden, and when he came out of his shell, he was entirely different." Honey Bea's face beamed as she told me the story.

One year, Honey Bea discovered she had cancer. Unfortunately, the cancer developed very fast, and she went downhill quickly. At the same time, her elderly mother who lived with her died, and Honey Bea literally got off her deathbed to play for the funeral. It was not long afterward that another organist played for Honey Bea's funeral. At her funeral, several of her Hispanic students took part in the service and, with tears in their eyes, recited the Lord's Prayer in Spanish.

Called to Play the Organ

The person who played for Honey Bea's funeral was Wanda Call, a member of the church whose husband John was an ordained minister, serving as a pastoral counselor. Wanda left her pew sitting position and became the new organist of the church. She was still organist when I retired many years later.

When I was in seminary, one of the "old ministers' tales" (as opposed to "old wives' tales") was that the choir is the war department of the church and the organist is the top sergeant. Nothing could have been further from the truth as far as Wanda was concerned. She was a kind person with a pleasing personality. She also was a fine organist...much finer than could be displayed on our old electronic organ. Years later when Hattie Mae Hoskins donated money for a new state-of-the-art organ that was tuned to our sanctuary, someone commented one Sunday, "Wanda, that postlude was wonderful. Why didn't you ever play it on the old organ?"

Wanda simply replied, "I did."

In recent years, contemporary worship services have become popular, and electronic guitars and drums have been added to the worship services in many churches. Some people have even said that the organ is now obsolete. I am always open to new ways of worship, and whatever is helpful for folks to feel closer to God is good, but for me a Bach prelude or a Mozart sonata on the organ with a competent organist on the organ pew will never go out of style.

17

The First Women Elders

In 1979, two women were elected as elders at First Christian Church in Duncanville, Texas. Today, this may not sound earth shaking, but when I began my ministry almost half a century ago, a woman elder was a rarity, if she existed at all. For the most part, it was taken for granted without question that elders were men.

If you are a member of the Christian Church (Disciples of Christ), you know the importance of the elder, and you can skip this paragraph. If you are not a member, let me explain that the office of elder is the highest lay office in the Christian Church. The elders (usually two at a time) stand behind the communion table every Sunday and pray over the communion. It is a highly respected spiritual office. At First Christian Church in Duncanville, elders are elected by the congregation for a three-year term and are ordained with a service called "the laying on of hands," which is similar to how ministers are ordained. Each elder is assigned a number of families in the church to contact each month, to see if they have prayer requests or other spiritual needs. The elders take communion to shut-ins and to members in the hospital. They also meet together once a month for mutual support and spiritual enrichment. It is a close-knit group.

When the possibility of women becoming elders was discussed, many had reservations. Some of this was probably the old adage "But we have never done that before." Church is a conservative institution, and often change comes slowly. There were also some questions among the elders themselves: "We have such a close-knit group. What will adding women to the group do to that?" However, there were also those in the congregation who felt strongly that there was no theological reason why women should not be elders. In fact, they said there were good reasons why women should be elders. One of the main duties of an elder is to nurture, and women have traditionally been the nurturers in our society.

It was never actually stated this way, but I think in the minds of many it was thought, "Well, let's try it as a kind of experiment, and see what happens." What happened first was that the two women elected, Lorraine Turpin and Bobby Dean, took the position of elder very seriously. Lorraine shared with me that being elected as elder was the highest honor of her entire life.

In the three years of their term, neither of the two women elders missed a single meeting or assignment. They were nurturing to their assigned families, and they faithfully took communion to members in the hospital. It was as if they knew that all eyes would be on them, and how they performed would influence whether or not women would continue to be considered for the eldership.

As far as the question of how women would affect the closeness of the elders themselves, if anything, the group got closer. A lot of the credit can be given to Lorraine and Bobby who were warm and supportive, but credit also needs to be given to the men who were open and accepting.

The experiment turned out to be a great success. Soon, the congregation added Roberta Smith, Frances Langford, and other women to the eldership. When I retired, it was generally accepted that there would be an equal number of women and men as elders.

18

God Bless the Youth Sponsors

Conventional wisdom says that the youth are the future of the Church, and if the Church does not pay attention to its youth, the Church may not have a future. I think there is truth to this, and for that reason, I have always put an emphasis on youth ministry. The first church I served after I graduated from seminary was a large church, which called me to be a youth minister. Youth ministry there involved developing programs for several youth groups and spending a lot of time with each young person during this impressionable and formative stage of life. It was a demanding task, but I could spend my full time doing it, since there was a senior minister to take care of the other aspects of the church.

Years later, when I was called to "my own church," as the saying goes, I was responsible for all aspects of church ministry and, therefore, could not spend all my time with the youth. Still feeling the importance of this ministry, I recruited youth sponsors from the congregation. My hat is off to those many personalities in the pews who served as youth sponsors over the years. They gave up every Sunday evening and often all weekend, not to mention the time for youth retreats and mission trips during the summer. Yet, these hearty souls didn't approach this task as a heavy burden that "somebody has to do," but rather met it with enthusiasm, a willingness to serve, and a good sense of humor.

These important qualities were often combined in a husband-and-wife team. For example, on a youth trip to San Antonio with Mike and Cindy Bingham as youth sponsors, Cindy made sure the youth saw and appreciated the five historical missions in San Antonio, while Mike made sure they also had fun.

A Fish Story

Mike Bingham was a tall man with a smile as warm as a Texas sunrise, a quick wit, and a sense of humor that wouldn't stop. He had a way of challenging the young people to think and to read between the lines of what is written and what is said. He always made a game of it. For example, when the youth group was planning an all-day fishing trip, he announced, "I'll bet that I can bring in the biggest fish of the day. I challenge every one of you."

Throughout the day, every time someone caught a fish, he or she would run over and compare it to what Mike had caught. Finally, near the end of the day, someone caught a fish that was bigger than anything Mike had in his bucket. As all the kids were gloating, Mike went to an ice chest in his car and brought out a huge fish he had purchased at a fish market. "But that doesn't count!" they all said. "You didn't catch it."

Mike smiled and replied, "Remember exactly what I said. I didn't say 'I'll bet that I can catch the biggest fish of the day.' I said, 'I'll bet that I can bring in the biggest fish of the day.' Always listen to what is said."

A few years later, one of the students from the group decided to enter law school. He told me he began thinking about that profession because of Mike's challenge to be precise and to think clearly.

Fun at the Beach

Stanley and Carolyn Scott, with David and Sandra Freeman, made a good youth sponsor team. The gals were good mamas for the kids, and the guys excelled with their combined senses of humor.

Stanley had one of the loudest and the most infectious laughs in the congregation. When I attempted humor in my sermon, I always hoped Stanley would be present, for his reverberating laughter would give everyone else permission to laugh. He brought this laugh and his sense of humor to the youth group.

One weekend the youth group went to Galveston, Texas, near the Gulf of Mexico. As the group set out to go to the beach, one of the boys began bragging about how he was going to pick up some girls. He kept saying, "Where are the girls? Bring on the girls!" As they got to the beach, Stanley noticed a couple of college girls by the soft-drink stand. Without anyone in the youth group noticing, he said to the girls, "Excuse me. I'm one of the sponsors of a church youth group down here for the weekend, and we have one boy who thinks he's God's gift to women, and won't stop bragging. I'll be glad to buy each of you a hot dog and a Coke if you would go over and give him a rush." The girls agreed, went up to the kid, and started flirting with him. Immediately, his macho exterior began to deflate, and his responses became one-word sentences.

"How are you doing, big boy?" one of the girls said.

"Ah...ah...okay," was the hesitant response.

"We're having a party up at our place," she continued, "...would you like to come?"

Looking straight ahead, he slowly mumbled, "Ah...ah...I've got to stay with the youth group."

You could hear Stanley's laugh all over the beach.

More than Fun

The youth program was much more than entertainment, however. With youth sponsors as leaders, the young people did many projects that reflected care and concern for others, especially others less fortunate. At nursing homes, they visited with the people, read to them, sang to them, sometimes laughed with them, and led worship services for them. They took on projects with older people who were still in their homes and needed help with such things as changing light bulbs or doing minor repairs. Every year there was a mission trip. On several mission trips, they worked with Habitat for Humanity, in which the youth took part in helping to build houses for lower-income families. They went to an Indian mission in New Mexico and helped with building projects there.

The youth, then, are not only the Church's future, but they are also an important part of the Church's present. In addition, the youth sponsors who work with them and lead them deserve a special place on the other side of the Pearly Gates.

19

Baptized in the Water

In the course of my ministry, I have baptized over 500 people. In our denomination, we practice believers' baptism by immersion. It is a dramatic service—one you never forget. Most of the people I have baptized have been young people who have gone through the Pastor's Church Membership Class, which I taught every Lent. It was exciting to experience those young minds asking probing questions and eagerly anticipating their baptism. It was also rewarding to watch them grow up, become more active in the church, get married, and then to baptize their children.

Those who went through the sacrament of baptism were not only young people, however. I baptized many adults who came later to the faith. One of the adults requested to be baptized in "living water" rather than in the baptistry of the church. On a cool September morning, we went to a local lake where he was baptized in the not cool but cold water. It was such a moving experience that the deacon who went with us decided to be rebaptized at the same time.

This incident reminded me of an experience I had years earlier when I led a church group to the Holy Land. As we stopped by the Jordan River, there were three groups of people being baptized by their ministers. There was an African preacher, a Jewish-Christian minister, and a Caucasian pastor.

At the conclusion of the service, the ministers rebaptized each other.

On a later trip to the Holy Land with my minister friend, David Worden, we echoed that earlier occasion by giving our people the opportunity to renew their baptism vows in the Jordan River. The event was dramatic in itself, but it was even more so as we witnessed a white dove, which is a symbol of the Holy Spirit, fly overhead.

Let me add a footnote here about the word "rebaptism." Theologically, I believe a person needs to be baptized only once. But just as persons may wish to renew their marriage vows in a special service, so might Christians renew their experience of baptism in a service of rededication. It was an extraordinary experience to hold such a service in the river where Jesus himself had been baptized.

A Funny Thing Happened on the Way to the Baptistry

Even sacred rites have their humorous moments. Once, when I had lunch with a group of ministers, we each shared some lighter incidents about baptism. One minister told of the difficulty of baptizing a three-hundred-pound man. Another told of baptizing a young person who was so short that her head was barely out of the water as she stood in the baptistry, and when he immersed her, her feet came flying up out of the water. Another told of a young person who was more impish than serious, and as the minister lowered him in the water, he broke loose and began swimming underwater. I told the story of my first baptism out of seminary, and how I forgot to take my watch off. I noticed it just as I was lowering the person into the water. (Too late!)

This reminded me of a story told by one of the early ministers on the frontier. As the minister was about to baptize someone in the river, the man said, "Wait! I forgot to take my wallet out of my pants."

The minister replied, "Leave it there. I need to baptize your money too."

As we continued with stories, I told of my first baptism at Duncanville and using the fishing waders left by the former minister. Quickly I discovered why he left the waders and didn't take them with him. They leaked. As I stood in the baptistry, baptizing a dozen young people, one at a time, I felt the water slowly rising inside the waders.

At that point in the sharing of stories, a woman minister in the group said, "I had that happen to me once." Then she added, "Have you ever tried to change clothes quickly while taking off wet pantyhose?" That stopped the conversation, and we all agreed that she had won the prize for the best story.

Out of the Mouths of Babes

Even though there are humorous moments, baptism is a sacred occasion and a meaningful experience. An example of an expression of this is something written by my son, Ryan, after he was in the sixth-grade Pastor's Church Membership Class. His English teacher in school gave an assignment to write about a meaningful experience. He wrote about his baptism. Here is a portion of what he wrote: "As my dad lowered me into the warm sacred water of the baptistry, I felt my body relax as if I were resting in the arms of angels. I felt the love of God surround me, telling me that I would never be away from His love and care. It was the most meaningful thing that has ever happened to me!"

20

The Welcome Table

Holy Communion or The Lord's Supper is unique in several ways in the Christian Church (Disciples of Christ). Whereas many churches have communion once a month or even less often, we in the Christian Church celebrate communion every Sunday. Whereas in some churches only an ordained minister can serve communion, in the Christian Church it is a combination of lay and clergy. In the Christian Church, we practice "open communion," which means you do not have to be a member of the church to receive communion. If you believe in Jesus Christ, you are welcome at the communion table.

Alexander Campbell, who was one of the founders of our denomination, grew up in a church where you had to check with the minister and get a token in order to receive communion. As he struggled with his faith, he came to believe that no one should decide who can or cannot receive communion. The invitation comes from Christ himself. One Sunday, as he stood waiting to present his token to receive communion, with trembling hands he dropped the token and left the church. Later, as a minister, he practiced what the Christian Church has come to call "open communion."

The reason for these two introductory paragraphs is to state and to emphasize how important communion is in the Christian Church (Disciples of Christ).

I can remember as a small child sitting with my parents in church every Sunday and watching them partake of communion. With how seriously they did this, it seemed to me that this was the most important part of the worship service. As the communion tray was passed, my dad would hold the tray while my mother took out one of the small wafers, and then he would take one. They each took a small cup from the tray, held it as they bowed their heads, paused, drank it slowly before replacing it, and then the tray was passed by me to the next person in the pew.

I was eight years old when I was baptized and received my first communion. I'm sure I did not understand the full meaning of communion, but who really does? Communion is a holy mystery and involves faith and deep feelings, as well as intellectual understanding. All I knew was that I felt I was now a part of something much greater than myself.

After I was ordained, I served as the youth minister in Warren, Ohio, and I led the youth group on a three-week mission trip to Quebec Province in Canada. We built an outdoor chapel for a summer camp that was set up for underprivileged kids. This project involved clearing a path to the area in the woods where the chapel was to be, felling trees, and using the trees to make log benches. Finally, we split apart the trunk of a large tree, and used both halves to make a communion table, which became the worship center at the front of the chapel.

When the project was finished, all the summer campers gathered for the dedication of the chapel. The youth group prepared and led a special communion service. Many of them said this communion service was the most meaningful part of the whole venture. Two of the young people in the group went on to become ministers.

A Lighter View of the Holy

As important and holy as communion is, there have been some amusing things happen during the service, and to share these does not distract from the importance or holiness of communion. I believe God has a sense of humor, and perhaps even God was amused at some of these incidents.

One Sunday, as I stood behind the communion table with a lay elder on each side, one elder reached to take off the lid from one of the communion trays and accidentally dropped it. The lid made a loud crash as it hit the communion table, breaking the meditative silence, as it hit the floor and rolled down the three steps of the chancel. It continued to roll down the center aisle, and with all eyes on the lid, it finally came to rest about five rows back. After a pregnant pause, someone in the fifth row picked it up, walked gently to the communion table, and with a slight grin, handed it back to the immobilized elder.

Another incident involved the contents of the communion cups. In our church, we use grape juice. A deacon prepares the communion by filling the little cups in the trays and places the trays in the refrigerator to be taken out just before the service on Sunday. On one occasion, a new deacon prepared the communion on Thursday, but omitted the step about the refrigerator. It was summer, and as the trays sat in the Texas heat for three days, the result mimicked the story in the second chapter of the Gospel of John, as the grape juice turned into something else. No one was aware of what happened until the partaking of the cup, but it was interesting to see the reactions on different faces: some solemn, some with a surprised grimace, and one with a smile and a joyful "mmmm!"

Perhaps the most amusing story about the communion service happened to me. At the beginning of the service I stand behind the communion table, break the communion bread, hold up half a loaf in each hand for all to see, as I recite the Words of Institution (I Corinthians 11:23–26). Just as I held up the bread, a fly lit on my nose. There are jokes about the fly on the minister's nose, but this was not a joke. What to do? It is amazing how many thoughts can go through your mind in an instant. Both hands were full, and I certainly didn't want to wave off the fly with communion bread. I didn't want to blow upward from my mouth, for the mike would pick up the sound. To wiggle my nose would have looked like something out of the old television show *Bewitched.* So, I thought, *Probably no one can see the fly anyway. Just leave it alone, and it will go away.* With that decision, I opened my mouth to recite the Words of Institution, and as I took a breath inward before speaking, the fly also went inward. For an instant, I froze. Then as a true professional and hopefully without any change of expression, I continued with the Words of Institution. Later, I discovered I was wrong about my earlier thought that probably no one saw the fly. Jack Bullock, who was sitting in the choir close to me, said he laughed so hard he almost fell out of his pew.

Something Special

Except for occasional incidents such as ministerial flies or grape juice turning into wine, communion remains a hallowed and significant service. I have never lost that special feeling I had when I took my first communion at the age of eight. For the forty-three years I stood behind the communion table each Sunday, the service never became merely routine. Although I spoke those words hundreds of times, the Words of Institution continually remained fresh as they invited the personalities in the pews to come to the welcome table.

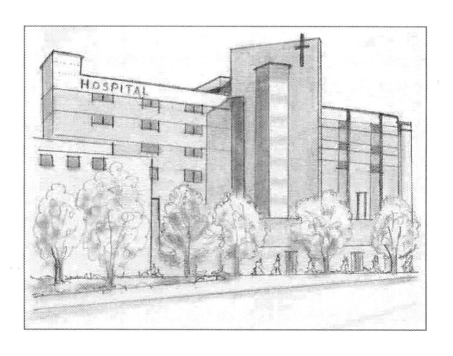

21

The Hospital Pew

You don't normally think of hospitals as having pews, but it is certainly true that the personalities in the pews often find themselves in the hospital. I feel that one of the most important ministries a pastor performs is visiting in the hospital. However, just as important are the visits that laypeople make to the hospital.

In every church I served, there were people who took it upon themselves to visit members who had to go to the hospital. In addition to individuals who called on their own, we had an elders' shepherding program. Each elder was assigned a portion of the congregation to be in his or her flock, and when someone from the flock went to the hospital, the elder would go see that person and offer a prayer.

I discovered for myself how meaningful these hospital visits were when I was scheduled for surgery, and one of the elders came to the hospital at 6:30 in the morning to have a prayer with me. Elders also often sat with family members while their loved ones were in surgery. I remember one elder who took off work in order to do this. When our daughter had ear surgery (also very early in the morning), one of the elders came to sit with my wife and me until the doctor came out and said everything was all right.

Elders not only visited, but they also took communion to those in the hospital. Often an elder who was serving behind the communion table on a Sunday morning would take some of the communion bread from the service to the hospital. This way the person in the hospital could partake from the same loaf as everyone else in the church family.

So, if the pew is the place where people sit during a church service and receive communion, and a person sitting in a hospital bed receives communion, then that hospital bed truly becomes the hospital pew.

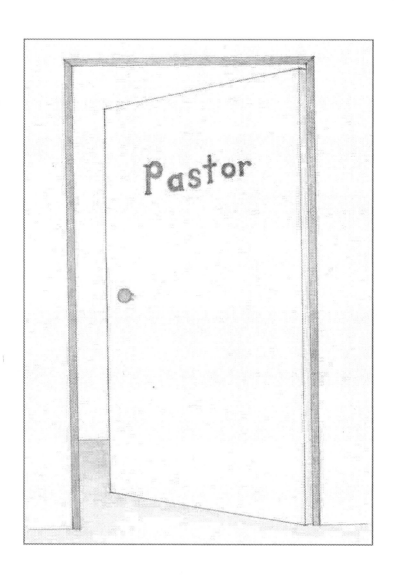

22

The Counseling Pew

The title of this chapter is perhaps a bit of a misnomer, for pastoral counseling usually doesn't take place in the pew, but rather in the pastor's study. However, misnaming probably isn't what might capture your attention at this point. Your question might be, "Is he going to write about the personalities in the pews and their counseling problems?" Such a disclosure would probably cause worry and anxiety for some and eager morbid curiosity for others. However, let me allay both fears and hopes. I do not intend in any way to reveal secrets that may have been shared with me in a counseling situation. I know things about many of the personalities in the pews that will go unspoken to my grave, and I'm certainly not going to reveal them in print. Even my wife is not privy to such things.

Incidentally, my wife, Gloria, shared with me that a member of the church happened to see a couple going into my office, and asked Gloria, "What's going on with (she named the couple)? Are they having problems?" Gloria answered that she didn't know, since I don't share such things with her. Gloria told me, "I think she was a little upset because she didn't find out anything, but then that's her problem."

I have always been greatly concerned about the privacy and anonymity of parishioners who come to see me. I even changed the plans for the new offices in the building project of 1988. The original plans put my office behind that of the secretary. Many offices are that way, but it would have meant that anyone would have had to go past her to get to me. I changed it so my office was off by itself at the end of the hall, where anyone could enter anonymously.

Counseling is an important part of what a minister does, and it definitely affects the lives of many. There is pre-marital counseling, post-marriage counseling, divorce counseling, bereavement counseling, and just plain old "I've got a problem, Pastor. Can I see you a minute?"

At one point in my seminary training, I thought about becoming a specialist and being a pastoral counselor. There are churches that have pastoral counselors as specialists on the staff. I took all the courses Yale Divinity School offered in psychology and counseling, and I spent one year as chaplain-intern at Elgin State Mental Hospital. This intern year was particularly helpful in my counseling training, because in a mental hospital you see personal problems in the extreme. For example, everyone gets "blue" occasionally, but the extreme of this is a full-blown state of depression. People in mental hospitals are not so different from people on the outside. Often they have the same kind of problems people on the outside have, but carried to the extreme. Seeing the extremes can help a pastor in a church recognize and deal with problems before they get to that extreme.

Ultimately, I decided to be a "generalist" rather than a "specialist," and chose to become a pastor, who does counseling but also does everything else in the church. However, as I half jokingly said to my congregation, "My experience and training in a mental hospital helped me to deal with you all."

The last word here is that counseling is a very important part of ministry. There is hardly anywhere else in our society where a person can get counseling help "right now" simply by knocking on a door. A good pastor is always available. Counseling may not take place directly in the pew, but it certainly affects the lives of the personalities in the pews.

23

For Better or For Worse

After I graduated from seminary and was ordained, I looked forward to performing my first wedding ceremony. There is something special about "firsts." I anticipated marrying a young couple that had grown up in the church—perhaps the daughter of one of the key leaders of the church. I could imagine later baptizing their children after they started a family, watching them celebrate each anniversary and, years later, remembering them as the couple in the first wedding I performed.

However, my first wedding was not what I anticipated. The people were not members of the church. In fact, they weren't members of any church. They just wanted to find a minister—any minister—who would marry them. They reluctantly sat through a pre-marriage counseling session as if to say, "OK, if this is what we have to do to get married, we'll do it, but let's get it over with." They stood in front of the sanctuary with a couple of friends. They said, "I do," kissed, left, and I never saw them again.

In the years to come, I did marry couples who were raised in the church, baptized their children, and celebrated their anniversaries, but this was not the case for my first wedding.

Two Truths

Over the years, I have discovered there are two things that are true about almost every wedding: the bride is always beautiful; the groom is always nervous. Grooms may be calm and cool during the counseling sessions, and even during the rehearsal, but at the wedding, their demeanor changes. They begin to pace back and forth, take several trips to the water fountain, and as we wait in the hall for our cue to enter the sanctuary, at the last minute I hear, "Do I have time to go to the restroom?" On one occasion, I thought I had discovered the exception to the rule. As we waited in the hall before the service, the groom was as calm and cool as a root-beer float. He even cracked a couple of jokes. Then about two minutes before the beginning of the service, he began to shake, and said, "I think I'm going to be sick!" It is one of life's little mysteries. It even happened to me. I entered the ministry single. Yet, even though I had been through many wedding services as a minister, when it came my turn to face the altar, I joined the ranks of grooms who were nervous just before the service.

A Few Faux pas

Except for not starting on time, most weddings go off without a hitch, but sometimes there is something that brings a grin from my memory. There was the time the groom was so nervous he couldn't repeat the vows. I always said them in little bits and pieces to make it easier to repeat, but this groom just couldn't pick up the pieces. I said them once, and he looked blank. I repeated them, and finally he muttered something that I took as vows. Then it was the bride's turn to repeat the vows. She had laryngitis, and when she moved her lips, no sound came out. I assured myself that they both made their vows in their hearts, and if God heard them, it should be good enough for the state of Texas, so I pronounced them married.

Brides and grooms are not the only ones with faux pas. At one wedding, when I asked, "Who gives this woman to be married to this man?" instead of answering, "Her mother and I," the father of the bride made a Freudian slip and responded, "My mother and I."

The most interesting faux pas I have experienced was by a minister who shared a wedding service with me. His niece was the bride, and three months before the scheduled wedding ceremony, she discovered she was pregnant. (This was over forty years ago, when such a situation was still embarrassing. Today, unfortunately, it is almost "ho hum.") The father of the groom, who was also a minister, married them in his living room immediately after he discovered that the bride was pregnant, but they planned to go through with the ceremony three months later. The father, the uncle, and I were all part of the service. At the end of the ceremony, the uncle, who didn't write his prayers, but prayed from the top of his head, gave the closing prayer that said, "Bless, O Lord, this marriage which has been consummated before us." (I think he meant "consecrated.")

At several weddings, the young ring bearer got cold feet at the last minute and wouldn't go down the aisle. After this happened the first time, I suggested to everyone that the ring on the pillow be a fake and that the best man hold on to the real ring. I also suggested that a very young flower girl not stand with the wedding party during the service, but rather be seated after she went down the aisle. I made this suggestion after one young flower girl constantly wiggled as she stood with the wedding party, and then turned and announced to the congregation that she had to go to the bathroom.

Another interesting situation happened when a bridegroom came down with chickenpox a couple of days before the wedding. By the time of the service, he stood in front of the altar in a tuxedo with his face completely "poxed out." After the honeymoon, the predictable happened: the bride came down with chickenpox.

I wrote earlier that most weddings don't start on time. On one occasion that happened in the extreme. It was an outdoor wedding timed to begin just after sunset, but the bride's hairdresser came late, plus the fact that the hairdressing took longer than anyone expected. We kept getting reports, "Just a few more minutes," but "a few more" turned into several more "few mores," and in the end, the ceremony took place over an hour late and in the dark.

The bride's sister was the maid of honor, and when she planned an outdoor wedding in her father's backyard, I reminded her to be sure the hairdressing situation didn't happen again, or we would have another service in the dark. She assured me that everything would be fine. At the time set for the wedding, the bride was ready on the dot, and it seemed everything would be fine, as she had said. However, it was not to be. A member of the family who was driving in from out of town hadn't yet arrived, so, once again, the ceremony was held up as darkness approached and finally came. This time, however, another dimension was added. This family member brought his dog. He locked him in the house, but the dog found a window near the backyard and howled during the entire service.

Up Close and Personal

Apart from the occasional funny incidents, weddings are beautiful and sacred events. In my forty-three years of ministry, I married hundreds of couples, but the ceremony never became for me merely a routine service. It is a privilege to stand close to a couple, witness their vows to each other, and ask God's blessing on their marriage. Whether there is a large wedding party with the sanctuary full or just the bride and groom alone standing before the altar, that special sacred moment is a treasure to be held in the memory of the couple and in the heart of the minister who married them.

Rest in Peace

24

From the Pew to the Gravesite

The first funeral I performed was for a patient at a state mental hospital where I served as a chaplain intern. The funeral director, who had a contract with the state for indigent funerals, picked me up and drove me to the gravesite. The coffin with the deceased lay in the back of the station wagon. When we arrived, two patients and an orderly from the hospital were waiting by the open grave. No one else was there. Neither of the two patients knew the deceased. They were there simply to carry the casket to the grave. As the station wagon came to a stop, the funeral director, who was smoking a big cigar, gently laid the cigar on the dash of the car as if to say, "This shouldn't take too long. No use wasting a good cigar by putting it out." I read the service from the service book provided by the chaplain's office. It took less than ten minutes. It was a cold winter day, but for me the experience was even colder.

I tell this story to emphasize something that I feel is very important at funerals—the presence and support of personalities in the pews when a fellow church member dies. Unlike my first funeral experience, usually there is a family member present who mourns the loss of a loved one. Certainly the minister needs to be physically and emotionally present, but just as important is the presence and support of a church family.

In every church I served, there were always members of the church who not only attended the funeral but who also did what they could to console and ease the pain of the bereaved. The women of the church would provide a meal for the family following the service. In many other ways, individual members would go out of their way to show support and concern. Time and time again, someone who had lost a loved one would say to me, "I don't know how I could have made it without my church family."

I remember one particular situation in which an elderly lady in the church died. She had been active in the church, but her only son was not interested in church. When the church members responded as they did with genuine sympathy and support, his attitude toward church changed. He became a member and became active—especially in the area of providing support for bereaved members.

Certainly, every Christian deserves a Christian burial, but as far as the funeral service is concerned, I feel it is mainly for the bereaved. Before the service, I always asked family members to share with me their memories of the deceased, and I incorporated these memories into the service. There is something healing about hearing in a funeral service your own memories. However, the service needs to be more than memories. It should offer the opportunity to hear the words of comfort and hope which our Christian faith can provide. These words are doubly helpful when they are backed up by the presence of personalities in the pews.

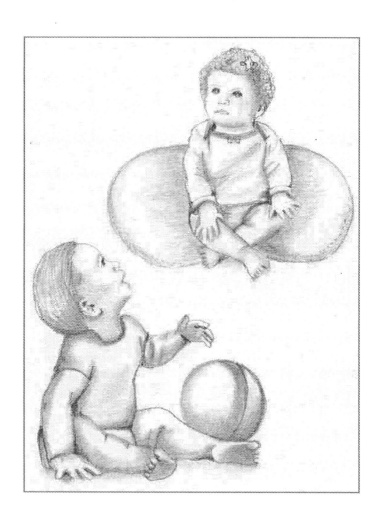

25

Let the Little Children Come

One of the church personalities who technically doesn't occupy a pew but is very important for those who do is the nursery attendant. There is no part of the church about which a young mother is more concerned than the nursery. I always told the Property Committee and the cleaning staff that the nursery needed to be spotless and cheerful. There is no better way to turn off a visitor than to have a crumby nursery. In Duncanville, we also had a cry room with one-way glass and sound piped in for those mothers who were nursing or just wanted to keep their babies with them.

In addition to the physical aspects of the nursery, the nursery attendant is also very important. Jesus constantly emphasized the importance of children: "Let the little children come to me...for it is to such as these that the kingdom of heaven belongs." (Matthew 19:14) "See that you do not look down on one of these little ones." (Matthew 18:14)

One of the nursery attendants who is outstanding in my memory is Clara Ables. Mrs. Ables was a quiet-spoken elderly lady whose demeanor exuded confidence and integrity. She shared with me that when she was very young her mother died. Her father felt he wasn't able to raise a young daughter and two sons, so he asked a relative to raise them. Mrs. Ables said that she appreciated what her father did because the people were kind Christian people, and she was glad to have been raised in a

Christian home. Everything about Mrs. Ables reflected this Christian upbringing.

Although Mrs. Ables lived in a very modest small-frame house and drove a twenty-year-old Plymouth, she was very generous with the church. I remember one time picking her up for baby-sitting, and as I went to the door, I saw her sitting at a table doing some figuring. She apologized for the delay, and informed me that she was figuring her tithe (ten percent of income). She said she had a small savings account and had just received the interest from it, and she wanted to be sure to figure ten percent of that, in addition to the ten percent of her Social Security check.

Mrs. Ables was more than just a nursery attendant. She was like a loving grandmother. She genuinely cared about the children and gave special attention to the young babies. She was the kind of person you could feel comfortable leaving your child with. My wife and I were happy to have her as a babysitter for our children.

After Mrs. Ables was no longer able to be the nursery attendant, there were others equally well qualified and who genuinely cared about the children. Among those were Daisy Winters and Mary Aguirre.

Recently, I was asked to lead a workshop on evangelism and getting new personalities in the pews. I shared with the group that there are many aspects to this, including advertising, calling, etc. I emphasized, however, that if you want young families to come, and if you want these families to come back, be sure the nursery and the nursery attendants are top notch.

26

The Family Pew

I always thought it was great to see families sitting together in the pews. This happened particularly on Mother's Day or Father's Day when I would often see four generations sitting together and taking up a whole pew.

I was a little sad that my parents couldn't be in church with me on those days, but they lived in Seattle, Washington, and a Social Security check didn't allow for flights to Texas. Imagine my surprise and joy when on a Saturday afternoon I walked into our living room to find my parents calmly sitting on the sofa. The church had flown them to Texas for the special occasion of my twenty-fifth anniversary as minister of First Christian Church in Duncanville. So, the next day, my parents, my wife, and our two kids made up three generations of my family sitting in a pew at church.

My father, who always had an interesting sense of humor, came to church, walking into Texas Rangers territory wearing a bold Seattle Mariners tie. During the announcement time of the service, I introduced my parents to the congregation and thanked them for the wonderful surprise of flying them to Texas. I also pointed out the Mariners tie, and then said, "That's OK, Dad," as I put on a red Texas Ranger baseball cap. I didn't leave it on for the service, however. Preaching in a baseball cap seemed to me a little inappropriate. There is a limit to how far team spirit should go in church. I remember reading about the frenzy in Denver when the Broncos were headed to the Super Bowl, and how a minister had to nix someone's suggestion to place an orange hanging over the pulpit. Fortunately, no one in Duncanville ever suggested hanging a Dallas Cowboys banner on the pulpit.

One other time, a faraway family member graced the church pew. This happened when I was serving as youth minister in Warren, Ohio. In 1962, I led the church youth group to the Seattle World's Fair. We stayed in churches along the way, and when we reached Seattle, we were hosted in homes of members of University Christian Church, where I had been ordained. My parents hosted one of the young people (Debby Downs), so my teenage sister (also a Debby) became a part of the visiting youth group. In fact, she became so much a part of the group that she and one of the boys in the group made more than eye contact.

When it came time for the group to head back to Ohio, my sister was sad to see the group—and especially the boy—leave, so I invited her to come back with us. She could continue to be with the group while we were on the road, and once we arrived in Warren, we could spend some time together as brother and sister. Since I had only a one-room apartment, the Christian education director in Warren offered us her home in the country while she and her husband were on vacation.

The second day we were in Warren, there came a timid knock at the door. It was the boy. "Is Debby here?" he inquired. "I was riding my bicycle and happened to be in the area." "The area" was six miles from town.

For a short time, then, my sister occupied a family pew, although the family was the youth group, and the pew was the last one in the balcony.

27

Each in Her Own Pew

There is a children's book entitled *Where's Waldo?* Each page depicts a different scene. It might be at the beach, at the circus, at a baseball game, or whatever, and each scene has hundreds of people in it. Somewhere in this crowded throng is Waldo, a skinny man with a top hat and always wearing the same clothes, which included a striped shirt. The point is to find Waldo in the crowd. When they were young, our kids loved the book, and so did my wife, Gloria, and I, because it kept the kids occupied for hours finding Waldo.

From my vantage point in the pulpit, if I wanted to locate a particular person in the pews, it was much easier than finding Waldo, for almost everyone sat in the same pew each Sunday. On my left, Mike and Carol Sink sat near the outside aisle seven pews back. On my right, Anne Hyman sat on the second pew from the front. The teenagers sat in the back pew on the right, and so forth.

I know why the teenagers sat where they did. They wanted to be as far away from their parents as they could, so they could punch each other and pass notes. I'm not sure about the psychology behind why others always seem to sit in the same pew. Maybe it's a stability issue or maybe a proprietary one.

In the church I served in Dayton, Ohio, there was an elderly lady who would ask people to move if they sat in "her pew." I discovered that her reasoning went back to the time the church was being built. In order to get finances to furnish the sanctuary, the minister had asked members to buy a pew. This lady took it literally, and when she gave her money, she felt that she owned her pew.

In the other churches I served, I didn't see a member ask someone to move. However, I did see situations where a visitor would sit in the pew where a member usually sat, and the member would hesitate, as if to say like the three bears, "Who's sitting in my pew," before moving on to sit somewhere else. Sometimes the member would say, "Are you a visitor today?" The visitor would answer, "Yes, am I sitting in your pew?" A little embarrassed, the member would say, "No, no, that's all right...welcome to our church."

In Duncanville, this pew sitting became more complicated when we went to two services. It was not so bad on a regular Sunday, but when the Dallas Cowboys played at noon, many of those in the late service would come to the early service, and that is when the pew jockeying would take place.

I have to admit that I was not immune to the pew-sitting situation. My wife, Gloria, sat on the left side five rows back from the front. We went to church separately since I had to be there for the early service, and she came to the late service. As the late service began, I would check to be sure she was there, because I always felt that I preached better when I could see her in the congregation. One Sunday I looked, and she was not in her pew. All kinds of thoughts went quickly through my head: Did she suddenly get sick? Did one of the kids get sick? Did she get stopped by the police for speeding on the way to church? For whatever reason, she was not in her pew.

Then we came in the service to the time for prayer requests. Sitting on the back pew, as if she had come in late and sat in the nearest pew, Gloria raised her hand and said, "I want a prayer of thanksgiving that I didn't get hit when the gear shift of your car came off in my hand and the car stopped in the middle of the street." When Gloria said "your car," she was referring to my 1929 Model A Roadster. That car never did like Gloria, and bad things often happened when she drove it, but that's another story.

"Where's the car now?" I asked from the pulpit.

"Don't worry," she answered. "It's not in the middle of the street. Some nice man pushed it to the service station close to the church."

So the mystery was solved. I'm still not sure if that was a real prayer request or if it was Gloria's way of saying, "I'm here, but I know you will be looking for me in the wrong pew."

28

More than Pew Sitters

In my forty-three years of ministry, I have witnessed from the vantage point of the pulpit a great number of personalities in the pews. The ones that stand out in my memory, however, are the ones who didn't just occupy a pew, but who stood up and took on positions of leadership and ministry. No church can survive or provide meaningful ministry, unless many of the personalities get out of the pews and give of themselves in leadership and service. When they do this, they truly bless the church.

A perfect symbol for this is the Cross itself, which represents among other things, self-giving.

In previous chapters, I have written about some of the personalities who were more than pew sitters. Here, I want to highlight a few more. I say "a few" because to list all those who were church leaders would read like an abbreviated phone book, and would be of no interest to anyone except those who saw their name in print. These few point out areas of important ministries and represent a host of those who have my undying appreciation for their dedication and leadership.

An extraordinary leader who comes to mind is Darrell Farris, who at one time was being groomed to run for governor of the state of Illinois. He decided, however, that his family was his first priority, and he didn't want to put them under the pressure that would ensue in such a political process. Instead, he turned his political talents and people skills into the service of the church. In many a board meeting, I appreciated Darrell's ability to think clearly and speak either calmly or forcefully, whichever was needed at the moment. Darrel and his wife, Vicki, were two of the most generous laypersons I have ever met. Vicki was one of the finest chairs of the elders I have ever seen, and she also chaired the Search Committee to look for a new minister after I retired. Darrell chaired the Stewardship Committee, which was responsible for financial campaigns and asking people to make pledges to the church.

Another person who served in the area of stewardship for many years was Ron Hundley. Ron, an attorney, frequently and generously shared his professional talents, and he enjoyed working in the area of stewardship. Many people shy away from such a position, not wanting to ask people for money. Ron and Darrell did it with such grace, integrity, and creativity that people responded cheerfully. And after all, the Bible says, "...God loves a cheerful giver." (II Corinthians 9:7) Ron's wife, Cheryl, was active in another way. As a nurse, she was a good medical resource person, and I remember her playing the piano for vacation church school.

Dale Ward could be a role model for a church treasurer, and he served amicably in that position for several years. I say "amicably" because the job of treasurer in a church is very difficult. When money is short, as it often is in a church, the temptation is to put on a negative persona, but Dale was always positive. He even brought cookies to the board meeting and passed them out before he made his treasurer's report. Later, Dale became chair of the elders, where his positive talents were again put to good use.

Cindy Hartgraves was for years one of the best elementary school principals I have ever seen, and she had great administrative talents and wonderful people skills. When she was asked to be vice chair of the church board, a position that after a year would move into board chair, she postponed a retirement move to the country in order to give of her talents for the next two years. It was fortuitous, because during her term, some very important decisions arose concerning the future of the church, and Cindy was the right person to be in the administrative seat.

Bob Stewart was certainly more than a pew sitter. Even though a member of the church, he was out of the pew more than he was in it because he was the area minister with responsibility for ministering to churches and ministers in the North Texas Area. Bob had the rare quality of being an excellent preacher as well as a good administrator. His unique position made for an interesting relationship between us. Since he was area minister, Bob was my minister, but since he was a member of the church I served, I was his minister. Bob also had a great sense of humor, and he liked to tease. An example was on my twenty-fifth anniversary celebration at the church. He preached the sermon that day, and knowing I had gone to Yale, he presented me with a Harvard T-shirt.

One of the marks of leadership and service is when someone sees a need and seeks to fulfill it. Such was the case when Judy Purcell led the church in adopting a refugee family. The father, who championed workers' rights in Poland, was arrested and was to be sent to a Soviet prison. Through delicate negotiations, the church was able to save him and his family by sponsoring them to come to America. The whole church responded under Judy's leadership, and it made front-page news in the *Dallas Morning News* and the *Duncanville Suburban*.

Another need in the church was a program for the retired and elderly. Thelma Fouts developed a daytime fellowship group and called it "Trendsetters." She chose a positive and non-age-oriented name in order to encourage anyone who needed such a group to attend. I can still hear in my memory her voice on the phone-tree, "Hello, Trendsetters. Don't forget our covered-dish luncheon and special program tomorrow."

Pat Carrithers had one of the brightest minds in the church. I loved to have him participate in the church school class I taught because he made such insightful comments. When he accepted a position of teaching the high-school class, I missed him in my class, but he was exactly what the high-school kids needed. Pat and his wife, Deborah, were artistically creative people who produced dramas in the church. In addition to several plays, they produced a medieval Christmas festival that was unique in the community. They also produced a video, *Come Meet our Church Family,* which we gave to visitors and prospective members.

David Bates, a retired Air Force colonel, had a big booming voice, which was great for dramatic effect, and he frequently took part in dramas at the church and in the community. David also added his voice to the choir, and he taught an adult church school class for several years.

Bob Cawthon noticed that visitors were often lost when they entered the church on Sunday morning. He took it upon himself to stand at the front door every Sunday to greet people and direct them to a church-school class or to the sanctuary. Church members began to refer to him as the leader of the Front Door Class.

In the area of worship atmosphere, Joan Crumroy went to seminary, got her master's degree in sacred design, and created huge banners for each season of the church year. Hanging in the sanctuary, not only were they beautiful as original works of art, but also they encouraged a worshipful attitude.

One of the best church libraries I have ever seen was created and maintained by Joan Crumroy and Sherry Perkins. They also constantly encouraged members to use the library.

Otto Crumroy was a retired Air Force auditor with strictness for church financial concerns. As such, he was one of the authors of *Church Administration and Finance Manual.* He had a softer side as well, however, with an interest in and a talent for classical music. He shared this talent by accompanying the organ with his viola during the early-morning worship service. He was also instrumental in arranging to have members of the New Philharmonic Orchestra of Irving to be a part of a special musical worship service at Christmas.

Sometimes accepting church leadership led to a new career. I asked Carol Sink to teach in Vacation Church School. She accepted and enjoyed it so much, she went back to college, got a teacher's degree, and became an excellent elementary-school teacher.

Leadership involved not only getting up out of a pew, but also enabling others to get into the pews. For several years Bob and Suszette White called on the visitors who came to church, giving them some homemade bread and encouraging them to come back to church.

Linda Higgins always brought friends to church. While most people would say something like, "I didn't make church last Sunday because we had friends visiting us," Linda would bring the friends with her. (Incidentally, when I retired, Linda gave my wife and me a trip to her favorite town, Savannah, Georgia. Connected with the trip, I read a book by John Berendt about the personalities in that quaint town, and that inspired me to write about the personalities in the pews.)

Robert Richards liked working with young people. He was like a big brother, and he was one of the first persons I thought of when one of the young people in the church needed a guiding hand. He and Stephen Lantrip worked together with the audiovisuals of the church, and they made opportunities for young people to work the sound system during the worship service. When Robert and Diane Richards began their landscaping business, they shared their talents with the church, and the beauty of worship was augmented with the beauty of plants and flowers around the outside of the church.

Gerald Hill was often my lunch buddy. Each of us was raising a teenage daughter, although Gerald was doing it as a single parent. Many a lunch was spent talking about the joys and challenges of parenthood. Several years after Don Cutler was killed in a tragic auto accident, I noticed Bobby Cutler and Gerald sitting together in church. It was not long before they not only joined pews, but joined hands in marriage. The whole church rejoiced in the union.

I mentioned Bobby Cutler's decorating talents in another chapter. Gerald's talent was in woodworking and fine restoration. The church benefited from this talent when the aging pews developed some structural problems, and Gerald moved from sitting in the pews to fixing the pews.

Another woodworker in the congregation was Jack Sanford. Jack developed a severe heart problem and underwent several operations, which meant he had to quit work. His wife, his family, his faith, and his sense of humor got him through. Although he couldn't work full time, Jack shared his woodworking talents with the church in many ways. One example was his making decorated wood crosses with "Bless this House" painted on each of them. When I was asked to perform a house blessing, I gave them one of these crosses. For the illustration which is at the beginning of this chapter and symbolizes the chapter, I expanded the idea to "Bless this Church," which is what the people did as they gave of themselves and their talents.

Earlier, I mentioned Jack's sense of humor. On one of our church anniversaries, we did a program in which members of the church played the parts of some of the early founders of the church. (The church was founded in 1893.) One of the early leaders was a carpenter and woodworker. Jack put on his woodworking clothes, and with his dry sense of humor, he stole the show as he brought laughter to the congregation as well as sharing some early First Christian Church history.

I have mentioned many times the importance of the elders. There have been many dedicated elders in the life of the church. An example of such dedication was Ronnie Perkins, who took off work in order to sit with the family of one of his flock who was having surgery.

If you were looking for a church-school teacher who was always positive no matter what, you would find that quality in Christine Kirtley. Her faith was warm and transparent as she also served in many other positions in the church. I especially appreciated her accepting the position of chair of the elders as I was about to retire. I had always had a close relationship with the elders, and as I retired, it was good to have her dedicated leadership in place.

Bill and Shirley Benesch were in their pew almost every Sunday, but their service to the church didn't stop there. They were active in the Visitor's Fellowship program, which reached out to bring others into the pews. Their service also reached beyond the local church. They were devoted lay leaders in Gideons International, which provides Bibles for hotels and motels all over the world.

Dosie Hulshouser was a little lady with a big talent. She had been a cook at the cafeteria in an elementary school. When she retired, she didn't hang up her pots and pans, but shared her cooking talents with the church. Every Wednesday for years, she prepared a dinner for the congregation, which gave opportunity for fellowship as well as a good meal. While most mass meals tend to be bland and almost tasteless, Dosie's meals were like home cooking. One of her specialty desserts was peach cobbler, which I really miss, but I'm sure the angels in heaven are enjoying it.

If members in the congregation went to the hospital, went to a nursing home, or became a shut-in, Leland and Ernestine Dixon were some of the first to go visit them. If someone needed a ride to church, Leland and Ernestine were the first to volunteer. They both were filled with good will and had a strong faith, which was reflected in their actions time and time again.

Taking care of the physical concerns of the church property is not an easy task. It would be easy for the chair of the Property Committee to feel overwhelmed or to get discouraged with all the concerns that arise. Gene Turpin and Merrill Womack are examples of people who handled it well. Gene was quiet and soft spoken, but he was very organized, and he delegated tasks well. Merrill had the right temperament for the job. He was dedicated and able, but he also had broad shoulders and a sense of humor, which helped him handle the many concerns and problems that came his way.

Fred Harris was one of the brightest young persons I had ever seen in the church. Not only was he smart, but he also had a warm and pleasing personality, and both young people and adults responded well to him. He was very active in the youth group and became one of the top leaders. I recognized early that he had great potential, and I encouraged him to consider becoming a minister. He took that encouragement seriously, achieved a good education, was ordained, and has served Christian churches in Ohio and Maryland.

Another bright young person was Ryan Hundley. Not only was he intelligent, but he was also an inspiration to all who knew him. Ryan had cystic fibrosis, a debilitating lung disease, which caused him to be in the hospital frequently. Many people in that kind of situation get bitter or give up. However, whenever I visited Ryan in the hospital, he was always upbeat and had a positive attitude. His goal was to get an education in the medical field so he could help others.

Several young people who were seminary students at Brite Divinity School at Texas Christian University were nurtured by First Christian Church in Duncanville. Although they had grown up in other churches, several of them chose to be ordained at First Christian Church. Among them were Carrell Still, Annell George, and Rachel Ganther. Brad Stagg was ordained in Houston, but he asked me to preach his ordination sermon. Three members in Duncanville who sought to move from the pew to the pulpit were Renee Hoke and Susan and Glenn Martin. Renee, who had had a successful career in the secular world, decided to go to seminary. When she graduated, she was ordained in Duncanville, and then became the first full-time associate minister of First Christian Church. Susan was ordained later, and at the time of this writing, Glenn Martin is a seminary student at Brite Divinity School.

Marty Williams was the only personality in the pew I didn't mind if he went to sleep during the sermon. He was a sports reporter for the *Dayton Daily News*. Often, he had to cover a Saturday-night game that went into the late hours of the night, and after that, he had to write and file his story. All of this resulted in Marty getting to bed in the wee hours of the morning. Yet, with very little sleep, he was always in church on Sunday morning. Occupying a pew on Sunday, however, was only the beginning of Marty's connection with the church. He and his wife, Shirley, served as youth sponsors, and Marty was the youngest person ever to be elected as an elder at Hillcrest Christian Church in Dayton, Ohio.

Everyone experiences cloudy days in life, but Willie Mae Fowler took on the role of a sunshine personality. When she heard that someone was sick or was having some problems, she would send them a cheery card with a personal note. She also sent cards to church members on their birthdays. After Willie Mae was no longer able to do this, Daisy Winters took up the sunshine role, and continued the card sending. Daisy added verses of Scripture to the notes she wrote. Even after I retired, I continued to receive kind notes from Daisy.

Barbara Detmore was the kind of person you would choose if you wanted someone who had good ideas, was well organized, and was thoroughly thorough. If you gave her a task, she would put her whole self into it. I asked Barbara to be in charge of the festivities for our centennial celebration at First Christian Church, and she did an excellent job.

Jack Bullock had the deepest voice of anyone I have ever heard. If James Earl Jones had developed a sore throat, Jack could have substituted for the voice of Darth Vader in *Star Wars*. His voice scared our daughter when she was a toddler, which made Jack sad, because he was a caring person and liked kids.

Jack sang in the choir, and sang bass an octave lower than anyone else. Jack also had other talents. In the military, he had been an interpreter, and he spoke Russian fluently. This gave me an idea for Pentecost Sunday. The Scripture for Pentecost tells how the Holy Spirit enabled the disciples to speak in tongues (other languages). For the reading of the Pentecost Scripture one year, I asked four persons to read in another language: Cristen Cawthon to read in French, Gloria Irving to read in German, Angela Irving to read in Spanish, and Jack Bullock to read in Russian. The only problem was finding a Russian Bible. French, Spanish, and German were not too hard to find, but Russian was a little more difficult. However, with the help of the Dallas Public Library, on Pentecost Sunday everyone in the church heard Darth Vader read the Scripture in Russian.

Theresa Dyer had been an army nurse, and had also served in the emergency room at a large hospital in Dallas. When she retired, she could have taken a well-deserved rest and merely occupied a pew on Sunday. However, she was at the church doing volunteer work in the office every week. Her comment was, "People don't realize what it takes to run a church. I'm glad to help out any way I can."

Theresa's attitude was reflected in the many personalities who not only sat in the pews, but who also got up out of the pews, took on leadership ministry, and helped the church be the church.

1 Thess. 5:18

29

That Special Ingredient

Why is it that some people can live meaningful and positive lives while others see only the negative and are always complaining? It's the old question, "Is the glass half full or half empty?" Those who see it half full are positive people. However, the question is, "How can you see it half full?" What is that special ingredient that helps you do this? In my forty-three years of ministry, I have discovered that special ingredient in the positive personalities in the pews is the ingredient of thanksgiving. Those who have been able to say "thank you" to others and especially "thank you" to God have lived more meaningful and more positive lives.

However, long before I discovered this in my ministry, the Apostle Paul discovered it in his ministry, and he wrote, "...give thanks in all circumstances." (I Thessalonians 5:18) "And let the peace of Christ rule in your hearts, to which indeed you were called in the one body. And be thankful." (Colossians 3:15) Even before Paul, the Psalmist said, "It is good to give thanks to the Lord." (Psalm 92:1) The Psalmist expressed this more than fifty times. There is something about thanksgiving that leads to a more positive attitude toward life and can also lead us closer to God.

A New Life

Rena Hanson did not grow up with a strong religious background. She was not necessarily an atheist, but she didn't think about God very much one way or the other. After she married and gave birth to her first child, she said, "It was such a moving experience to hold this new life in my arms. I had to have someone to thank...someone greater than myself...someone with a capital 'S.' This led me to my belief in God." Later, Rena became a director of Christian education, and I served with her in my first church.

A Beautiful Mind

Glenn Walser is a creative genius. He has the ability to imagine something, see it in three dimensions in his mind, and then create it. He has invented and manufactured machines that are now sold all over the world. He has reaped not only international recognition, but also great monetary rewards. But rather than taking personal credit for his talent and accomplishments, Glenn constantly says, "God has been good to me. I owe all my achievements to God, and I am eternally thankful for all the blessings I have. I can't thank God enough."

You might say, however, that it is easy to be thankful and have a positive attitude when things go well. What about when things do not go well? In an earlier chapter, I wrote about Jason Boles who at a very young age developed muscular dystrophy and progressively got worse until he could hardly move, and yet when someone tried to assure him that God would reward him, his response was, "He already has." It was his ability to be thankful to God for life itself that gave him his positive attitude.

A Communion Offering

Let me tell you another true story. Like the Walsers, there was another couple in the church who was economically well off. When the husband died, he left his wife with enough money to do almost anything anyone would want to do. However, not everything was rosy in this picture. The wife was also left with a mentally challenged son. As he was growing up, he had always been a challenge—doing such things as lighting the trash can on fire and putting the dog in the clothes dryer. As he grew older, he became harder to manage, and now she had to manage him alone. Almost everywhere she went, her son went along with her. The woman was a small, quiet person, and the son was big, demanding, and loud. If you saw her out and about or in church, it would be difficult to have a conversation with her because the son kept interrupting. In church, he sat next to her, and always had an extremely long list of names during the time for prayer requests.

Most people felt sorry for the woman and said such things as, "Poor lady. With her son like he is, it's got to be a real burden. I don't know how in the world she manages to be so positive."

One Lenten season, I developed a communion service to be held in the various homes in the congregation. One service was held each night during Lent with a dozen people attending. At one part of the service, I asked each person to share something for which he or she was thankful to God. This sharing of thanksgiving would be their offering to God as they took communion. The woman volunteered her home for one of the services, and as we went around the circle, people shared such things as being thankful for good health, good fortune, and good friends. When it came to the woman's turn, she said, "I am thankful to God for my son. We waited so long for a child, and I thank God for him."

People no longer questioned how she managed to be so positive. That special ingredient was thanksgiving.

A Beautiful Spirit

As Betty and Charles Wilkins stood in line to participate in a church project one Sunday, they talked about plans for a long-awaited trip. The next day Charles had a heart attack and died. There is no good way to lose a spouse. Some people watch their loved one die in inches. Others, like Betty, lose their loved one in an instant. Either way, it is one of the most arduous experiences that can happen to anyone. Psychologists have rated the various stresses in life on a scale of one to a hundred, and the highest level of stress (100) is the loss of a spouse. Not too many points below on the scale is the loss of a child.

Not long after Betty lost her husband, she watched her daughter die of cancer. Then, without warning, she had to deal with the tragic loss of her son—all of this in a relatively short period. How do you deal with such things? I have seen some people with such losses lose their faith and turn against God. Let me share with you some of the things Betty shared with me.

When her husband died, Betty said, "Losing Charles is like a nightmare. I will miss him terribly, but I'm grateful to God that I had him as long as I did."

When her daughter died, she said, "This is really hard. Parents aren't supposed to bury their children. It's supposed to be the other way around, but my daughter had cancer, and I am thankful she is no longer in pain."

When her son died, she said, "I don't understand why my son had to die, but I'm thankful he had a strong faith in God, and I'm holding on to that same faith to see me through."

In no way do I want to minimize the agony and loss that Betty must have felt, and she had tears in her eyes when she said those things to me. Yet, even in the midst of tragedy, she could be thankful to God, and that thankful faith did see her through.

A Meaningful Life

Life is fragile, and most of us find ourselves in the midst of loss and tragedy at some point in our lives. We cannot always choose what happens to us, but we can choose how we respond to what happens, and those who are able to recognize that special ingredient of thanksgiving are the ones who are also able to live more positive and more meaningful lives.

30

God's Greatest Gift to Me

Most people get to sit with their spouses in church. Each Sunday, I could look down from the pulpit and see couples and families sitting together in the pews. For forty-three years, I wasn't able to do that—except twice a year: on Youth Sunday and Women's Sunday. Of course, it would have looked funny to have my wife sit next to me up in the chancel in front of everybody. But, if she wasn't physically next to me, she always was emotionally, for my wife, Gloria, was the greatest support in my ministry.

Being the wife of a minister is not easy. She might as well have been sitting up there with me, for, in a sense, the wife of a minister is always in front of everybody. Living in the parsonage is a little like living in a cage at the zoo. Added to this, there are still people who feel like the church should be getting two for the price of one.

When I proposed to Gloria, she said, "But I have never taught Sunday school, or sung in the choir, and I can't play the piano."

I assured her that was not what I wanted to marry her for. I wanted her simply to be my wife. She said, "Yes." We were married in Kansas City, and our honeymoon consisted of driving from Kansas City, Kansas, to Duncanville, Texas, and stopping one night in Shangri-La, Oklahoma.

In the course of our twenty-eight years at First Christian Church in Duncanville, Gloria did teach Sunday school, and she did sing in the choir...but she never did play the piano. I need to say that these positions were not forced on her by the church or me. She freely chose them, and she says she enjoyed them.

Gloria also took on other areas of service and ministry. Our junior-high youth group was floundering with almost no one attending. She discovered the potential students, called each family, set up both serious and fun programs, constantly made contact with the kids, and ended with an ongoing group of fifteen to twenty. The group grew even larger, as many of the kids started bringing their friends.

Later, Gloria led the night circle of the Christian Women's Fellowship, and by using the same organizational techniques, she helped this group also to grow.

Gloria didn't want to accept any office or chair position or serve on the Official Board. For the most part, she worked behind the scenes. She didn't want to call attention to herself, but in a calm unassuming way, she performed a real ministry. As an example, she helped an African-American single mom who had six children. She, along with other friends in the community and church, helped the family from becoming homeless. She collected food for the family. She put appeals in the church newsletter, and people responded with furniture, a refrigerator, clothing, and bikes and toys for the kids. She then encouraged the mother and helped her get into nursing school, and she helped with transportation while the mom was in school.

Gloria was always the perfect hostess, having Visitors' Fellowships in our home frequently and having an open house at Christmas. Once, when the chair of the board came to our house for a meeting, Gloria had prepared some refreshments and left them on the table. He looked at this freshly baked offering and said, "Does your wife have a sister?"

Gloria provided the greatest support to my ministry by being a wonderful wife. In many ways, she was God's greatest gift to me. No matter how the day of ministry might go—an exhausting hospital call with someone dying, a long complicated board meeting, or some disgruntled parishioner—at the end of the day, I came home to love. There is an old country saying: "Kissin' don't last; cookin' do." Gloria was and still is an excellent cook, but after more than a quarter of a century of marriage, the kissin' is still there as well.

31

My Wife's Best-Kept Secret

At six-foot-three, Mike Sink was one of the most imposing personalities in the pews. With a quick glance, I could always tell if he was in church or not. He and his wife, Carol, always sat about seven pews back near the outside aisle, and as he sat erect, even if the pews in front of him were full, he stood out like a church steeple in a small village.

Mike and Carol had been members for almost a quarter of a century, and as I watched his hair and beard turn white, it only made him look more dignified. He had a love for the church and a respect for the ministry.

When I announced my retirement to take place in eighteen months, Mike secretly went to my wife and informed her that he wanted to do something special for me as a retirement gift. He had heard that I wanted a motor scooter.

In my college days, I had had a dream of getting a motor scooter and traveling all over Europe. The motor scooter part of that dream never worked out, but the desire never faded over the years. Mike could understand that because he had had a love affair with motorcycles in his own past, and he and I both shared the conviction that a mode of transportation was more than just a means of getting from place to place.

The problem was, just before Mike approached my wife with the motor-scooter idea, in anticipation of my retirement (and second childhood), I had already ordered and put a down payment on a motor scooter. When my wife reported this, Mike responded with a frown of disappointment and a query, "What, then?"

My wife didn't have to think long for an answer. She knew there was another dream I had. I had always loved sailing, and wanted some day to go sailing on a tall ship with multiple masts, and a plethora of sails. With the possibility of that "some day" actually coming to pass, Gloria gathered information from a company named Star Clippers, and gave the information to Mike.

The next eighteen months brought a flurry of secret meetings between Mike and my wife. He would catch her eye after church, and while I was shaking hands and talking with other personalities in the pews, they would dart off to the library or some church-school classroom, where he shared the progress of the project.

"I'm talking to several other people who are interested in being a part of this," he said at the first meeting. In subsequent meetings, decisions had to be made concerning what ship, what destination, and possible dates.

During this time, I started making retirement plans of my own for Gloria and me. I wanted us to spend several months as camp hosts in a state park in Colorado.

Gloria responded, "I don't want to make any plans for the first year after you retire. We need to just relax for awhile."

This confused me, because Gloria was always open and ready to go on new adventures. I learned later the reason for this statement. The date for the cruise had not been set, and she wanted to keep the calendar open.

On the last Sunday before my retirement, the church planned a big event with invited guests, many gifts, a catered dinner, the mayor giving me the key to the city, and all kinds of other happenings.

A couple of weeks after all the official festivities were over, Bob and Bonnie Cawthon invited Gloria and me for dinner. As we drove up to their house, I recognized other cars there, but I had no idea what was about to happen. The Cawthons often invited more than one couple to dinner, and I thought this was the case that night.

We had a tasty dinner. They all said how much they appreciated my ministry, and they wished for us a good retirement. Carol Sink wrote and read a poem. Then Mike stood up, looked at me, and announced that the group was sending Gloria and me on a cruise on the *Royal Clipper*—the largest sailing ship in the world with five masts and forty-two sails. The cruise to the Grenadines included stopping at Barbados, Tobago Cays, St. Vincent, Bequia, St. Lucia, and Martinique.

I was speechless. I realize that phrase has become a cliché, but for me it was literally true—which says a lot for a preacher. What made this gift extra special was that it was a genuine surprise. Surprise parties rarely are a surprise. Usually someone, without realizing it, lets something slip. In this case, for over a year, no slips occurred, and my wife, in all her excitement and anticipation, held the best-kept secret of her life.

For this most wonderful gift, I want to say "thank you" to Mike and Carol Sink and the following couples: Bob and Bonnie Cawthon, Darrell and Vicki Farris, Richard and Jean Griner, Brice and Cindy Hartgraves, Bill and Jeanette Kennedy, Stanley and Carolyn Scott, Glenn and Wanda Walser, Bob and Suszette White, and Bob and Ann Worsham.

32

Epilogue

The Other Side of the Story

I had a conversation about this manuscript with a member of the faculty at Brite Divinity School at Texas Christian University, and he suggested that I needed another chapter.

"You have written about the wonderful positive church people," he said, "but, what if people who read it say, 'That's not my church.' What about the personalities in the pews who are not so positive? What about the other side of the story?"

Another person suggested that I should write two parts to the book. On the front side, I could use the title *Personalities in the Pews*. I could turn the book over and, on the back, use the title *Personalities that are "Phew."* The two parts would meet somewhere in the middle. I decided against that suggestion, but something does need to be written that responds to the following real-life situations:

—The chair of the board who went through so many problems and so much negativity in his term that, when it was over, he didn't want to do anything in the church anymore.

—The young minister who began with great idealism and, after several churches, became cynical.

—The minister who said, "I had six wonderful years at that church." Then he added he had been there seven years, and the last year was anything but wonderful.

—The minister who had five members of his congregation come into his study one day and say, "We think it's time for you to leave—don't take this personally."

Two words need to be said here: one to congregations and one to ministers.

A Word to Congregations

Congregations need to know that being a minister is not easy. If a church has 300 members, in a sense, the minister has 300 bosses. Each of these bosses comes with his or her idea of what the church should be and what the minister should do. Most ministers are dedicated individuals, but it is impossible for a minister to meet all these expectations.

Congregations need to know that ministry is not just a popularity contest. Sometimes a minister may need to speak a prophetic word that some will not like to hear. As someone once said, "The task of the minister is to comfort the afflicted and afflict the comfortable."

Congregations need to recognize that every minister has strengths and weaknesses. Strengths need to be acknowledged and rewarded, while weaknesses need to be addressed with continuing education or by lay volunteers to fill in the gaps.

Congregations need to recognize that the minister is human and has the whole range of human feelings. It is unrealistic to strike out at a minister and expect him not to take it personally. Pray for your minister. The same can be said for lay leaders in the church. Pray for your leaders.

"As God's chosen ones, holy and beloved, clothe yourselves with compassion, kindness, humility, meekness, and patience. Bear with one another and, if anyone has a complaint against another, forgive each other; just as the Lord has forgiven you, so you must forgive. Above all, clothe yourselves with love, which binds everything together in perfect harmony. And let the peace of Christ rule in your hearts, to which indeed you were called in the one body." (Colossians 3:12–15)

A Word to Ministers

Early in my ministry, the General Minister and President of the Christian Church (Disciples of Christ) gave a talk to the young ministers, and said, "In your ministry two things will always be true: the church roof will always leak, and in spite of everything you do, you will be someone's favorite minister." I found both of these to be true, but he could have added, "In spite of everything you do, someone is not going to like you."

This can be a difficult thing for some ministers to accept. There is a part of us that wants to please everyone. There is also a part of us that thinks we can do it, and when we don't, we feel like failures. Ministers need to be realistic, and not be so hard on themselves.

Ministers need to realize that the congregation is made up of people who are human, and that they come to church with all their human problems. Often, people who are difficult or cause problems in church are reacting to something not even related to the church. A problem at work, a problem at home, or a health problem can cause people to strike out in the one place that can't fire them or reject them—the church.

Often, this striking out at the minister isn't personal. The minister happens to be in the place of leadership and authority, and here is where they strike out. To realize the dynamics of this can perhaps lessen the sting. However, it is always important that the minister responds in a way that makes communication and reconciliation possible.

Early in my ministry, I talked with a minister who had been in his church for thirty years. I asked him, "How do you stay in a church thirty years?"

He answered, "If there is some problem or some hard feelings, they know I'll be coming to see them."

The last thing I would say to ministers is constantly to tell yourselves whom it is you are really working for. The majority of people in the church are wonderfully positive people, but when someone is negative, strikes out, or is disappointing, don't let it cause you to become cynical. Keep that "just out of seminary idealism" by remembering that it is God for whom you are ultimately working. "For we are God's servants, working together; you are God's field, God's building." (I Corinthians 3:9) "Do not lag in zeal, be ardent in spirit, serve the Lord. Rejoice in hope, be patient in suffering, persevere in prayer." (Romans 12:11)

You also might want to write a book about the positive personalities in the pews.

Index of Personalities in the Pews

Ables, Clara, 113-114
Aguirre, Mary, 114
Bates, David, 128
Benesch, Bill, 131
Benesch, Shirley, 131
Bingham, Cindy, 68-69, 80
Bingham, Mike, 80
Blanchard, Susan (Susan Martin), 132
Blevins, Verba, 43-44
Boles, Buddy, 10
Boles, Christina Gonzalez, 10-11
Boles, Jason, 9-11, 138
Boles, Lyn, 10
Buckner, Annell, 27
Buckner, Jim, 27-28
Bullock, Honey Bea, 71-72
Bullock, Jack, 92, 133-34
Call, John, 73
Call, Wanda, 73
Campbell, Alexander, 89
Carrithers, Deborah, 128
Carrithers, Pat, 127-28
Cawthon, Bob, Acknowledgments page, 128, 148-49
Cawthon, Bonnie, 148-49
Cawthon, Cristen (Cristen Rocha), 134
Collins, Elizabeth (Elizabeth Daniel), 24-25
Collins, Lee, 22-25

Crumroy, Joan, 128

Crumroy, Otto, 128

Cutler, Bobby (Bobby Hill), 61, 129-30

Cutler, Don, 60-61, 129

Daniel, Bob, 57-58

Daniel, Elizabeth (Elizabeth Collins), 24-25

Daniel, Frances, 24, 57

Daniel, R.N., 24, 57

Dean, Bobby, 74, 76

Dean, Ray, 59

Detmore, Barbara, 133

Detmore, John, 58-59

Dixon, Ernestine, 131

Dixon, Leland, 131

Downs, Debby (Debby Harris), 118

Dyer, Theresa, 134

Farris, Darrell, 125-26, 149

Farris, Vicki, 126, 149

Faulkner, Bill, 33-34

Faulkner, Deb, 34

Fouts, Thelma, 127

Fowler, Willie Mae, 133

Freeman, David, 81

Freeman, Sandra, 81

Ganther, Rachel, 132

George-McLawhorn, Annell, 132

Graye, McKenzie (Debby Irving), 118

Griner, Richard, 149

Griner, Jean, 149

Hansen, Rena, 13-15, 138

Hardie, Catherine, 18-19

Hardie, David, 19

Hardie, John, 17-20

Harris, Debby (Debby Downs), 118

Harris, Fred, 48, 132

Hartgraves, Brice, 149

Hartgraves, Cindy, 126-27, 149

Higgins, Linda, 129

Hill, Bobby (Bobby Cutler), 61, 129-30

Hill, Gerald, 129-30

Hoke, Renee, 132

Hooper, T.W., 42-43

Hoskins, Hatie Mae, 59, 61, 73

Hulshouser, Dosie, 131

Hundley, Cheryl, 126

Hundley, Ron, 126

Hundley, Ryan, 132

Hyman, Anne, 121

Irving, Angela, Acknowledgments page, 37-38, 48, 60, 134

Irving, Debby (McKenzie Graye), 118

Irving, Gloria, Dedication page, Acknowledgments page, 6, 48, 99, 121-23, 134, 142-45, 147-49

Irving, Ryan, Acknowledgments page, 32, 48, 87

Kennedy, Bill, 149

Kennedy, Jeanette, 149

Kirtley, Christine, 130-31

Langford, Frances, 38-39, 76

Langford, Luther, 37-39

Lantrip, Stephen, 129

Martin, Glenn, 132

Martin, Susan (Susan Blanchard), 132

Matney, Mildred, 41-42

Perez, Jaime, 68

Perkins, Ronnie, 130

Perkins, Sherry, 128

Purcell, Judy, 127

Richards, Diane, 129

Richards, Robert, 129

Rocha, Cristen (Cristen Cawthon), 134
Sanders, Robin, Acknowledgments page
Sanford, Jack, 130
Scott, Carolyn, 81, 149
Scott, Stanley, 81, 149
Shinn, Stella, 4-7
Sink, Carol, 121, 129, 147, 149
Sink, Mike, 121, 147-49
Smith, Roberta, 76
Stagg, Brad, 132
Stewart, Bob, 127
Still, Carrell, 132
Turpin, Gene, 131
Turpin, Lorraine, 74, 76
Walser, Glenn, 138, 149
Walser, Wanda, 149
Ward, Dale, 126
Weatherly, Ernest, 1-2
White, Bob, 129, 149
White, Suszette, 129, 149
Wilkins, Betty, 140
Wilkins, Charles, 140
Williams, Marty, 132-33
Williams, Shirley, 133
Winters, Daisy, 114, 133
Womack, Merrill, 131-32
Worden, David, 86
Worsham, Ann, 149
Worsham, Bob, 149

Index of Scriptures

Psalms 92:1,   137
Matthew 18:14,   113
Matthew 19:14,   113
Romans 12:11,   154
I Corinthians 3:9,   154
I Corinthians 11:23-26,   91
II Corinthians 9:7,   126
Ephesians 4:26,   64
Colossians 3:12-15,   153
Colossians 3:15,   137
I Thessalonians 5:18,   136, 141

To order more copies of

Personalities in the Pews

(Stories of Inspiration and Humor)

Call Toll-Free
(877) BUY-BOOK

OR

www.EldonIrving.com

Also available as an eBook